A CELEBRATION OF
THE MIND

BY

DENNIS J. BOCK

PublishAmerica
Baltimore

ISBN: 978-1-4489-7278-4
PUBLISHED BY PUBLISHAMERICA, LLLP
www.publishamerica.com
Baltimore

Printed in the United States of America

To Esther and Robert

"To be a writer at all one must certainly have a split personality. But when it comes time to reach for your hat and take an airing, you've got to be certain that it's your hat, your own legs"

—*Henry Miller,*
"My Life as an Echo"

"To be born again, first you have to die."

—*Salman Rushdie,*
The Satanic Verses

1

Two weeks after I shot myself in the face I asked my brother if I was a bad guy. I was staring blankly into space or rather a spot on my freshly painted semi-gloss white wall in my room. The blemish on such a clean surface irritated me and I was too far away to recognize it as a fingerprint or a shadow. I mean I only painted the wall a couple of days ago.

My brother was seated in front of the computer, which was to my left as I laid on my bed. He encircled his hand over his head cupping it like a melon before letting out a heavy sigh. I turned my head and the computer screen was littered with words I couldn't read but I know what they said…Hey man, what up, whatcha doin. Nuthin'. Yea, me neither. Hold on, what, Reg just IMed me. With a twinkle sound, another Instant Message box opened up for him.

"Hello?" I spoke up. I didn't think he heard me. "Hello?"

Hi, he typed. "What?" he finally acknowledged to me.

"Do you think I'm a bad guy?

"What?! What kind of a question is that?" He kept typing away talking to whoever it was on the other side of the screen.

"I just want to know."

"I don't know. Do you feel like one?"

"That's a stupid question."

"So is the one you're asking!" He turned around. He stared at me. The light that hung from the ceiling dangled heavily in his eyes. His blonde curls that were once there now were little points of pine that shaped out his head with a glow from the screen that appeared saintly but those eyes said different; they said they were annoyed. The computer made that magical sound of a message arriving and he turned around. "And why did you paint these walls white? Why not something a bit different?"

"I don't know. I guess insanity's a good color for me."

He turned and looked at me out of the corner of his eye. Then he went back to concentrating on his computer conversations. It wasn't insanity that got me; all I wanted what was rightfully due me. I knew he would never know about what I did. Nobody would really. Anyway, it was done with. I got my life back. I wouldn't tell him though.

A long time ago, years gone by, I came up with the notion that I wanted to be a writer. Innocent thought from a boy of fifteen. Little did I realize that I was one already and all I was accomplishing was perfecting my craft. So each day passing on and on, I wrote a piece of poetry here and a paragraph set to nothing there. As a scientist creates a theory without the experiments have taken place, my creations were blibs on paper with no story. But continue on I did.

As time grew older, my paragraphs grew into pages. Pages were then laid out across my floor, all over the walls as I imagined a Burroughs wall would look like. A bit scatterbrained but with purpose. During my time in catholic high school before I reached my state of Burroughs, I had begun imitating other writers. My stages varied in length depending on how influential each writer meant to me. Shakespeare, I think, was the first that I started with, writing prose like it was dialogue. That quickly changed when I had an encounter with Poe and I wanted to be dark and mysterious but that was over and done within a year. Then it was Hemingway with a side of Fitzgerald. Then some Henry Miller was added to the mix. The longest reign I had were the existentialists who reminded me a bit like the romantics but the only difference was that tragedy was in acceptance rather than loss. So I went through them like the average man goes through socks trying to find the right fit for me, like Kafka and Camus; Zola and Proust (he's existential if you only look) and finally landing one that I felt close to, James Joyce. I lived with Joyce for about two to three years. Then something happened, I had to get a job.

Suddenly Joyce wasn't working for me anymore. I was working in a library as a page putting books away. Pay wasn't that great but I was surrounded by literature every day. Eventually, catching me reading almost daily, they fired me. So I tried my hand into something more professional. Hired as a bank teller work was progressing well when one day my drawer was under the amount it had to be and I was accused of stealing so I quit before they could call the cops. Not to mention that I saw the cute girl Nancy who sat next to me a week later on the street and told me they'd found the missing money on the floor and that I must've dropped it. Assholes. As a teller in another bank, my drawer was over the amount cause I had left deposits from the night before undone and put them with the next day's. So I quit there too and decided that banks were not the way to go.

As a workingman, or trying-to-find-a-job man, Joyce wasn't helping me hold a job or couldn't get me through the daily grief. I met with Miller again but only briefly. But as soon as I met Kerouac, Burroughs soon followed. Funny enough, I named my iPod Pantopon Rose. My favorite band was Steely Dan and I found a job as a porter in a somewhat large, decently sized company cleaning floors, toilets, windows and even the sink. It was great. Got a paycheck every week. Writing became more exciting and I felt invigorated and, with a valor in drudgery, my work expanded. Along with my work growth, my age increased coincidently so did maturity. My love life found a place in my artistic lifestyle, her name was Shusha. Her name referring to the place her family had come from. We had fun. Maybe my grass was green and I couldn't see it. It always had this path that I was on and I searched for something else. What really threw my life in a tailspin began only a few months before my abrupt strange question I put to my brother.

DECEMBER

Thanksgiving was now a memory and concentration on purchases for the upcoming Christmas began. I had saved some money to buy Shusha a petite chain with two dolphins facing head to tail circling and a ruby in the empty space between them. Was it necessary? No. Did I want to do it? Sure, it guaranteed playtime. Staring at the tiny object behind glass I could see her night black hair falling down as she would let it fly after I'd attach the delicacy on her and the contrasting ceramic ochre shade of her skin not unbreakable porcelain but soft as cotton as my lips would magically say the words Merry Christmas before appearing pursed and kissing the flesh. That bubble burst fizzing away into nowhere accepting oblivion as the lady in the horribly gentrified uniform handed back my plastic debit from her untimely sixty-ish wrinkled hand. I looked into those tired fifty-something green eyes in confusion.

"What's the problem?"

"I'm sorry sir but your card was not approved."

My right eyebrow raised itself as the left lowered to show that I did not comprehend what she was saying. Eyelids blinked rapidly for a couple of seconds until it rested on my card with my name on it to make sure it was mine and that she didn't mistake it for someone else's. You can never be too careful these days.

"What?"

"Your card was not approved."

"Yeah, I know but why not?"

"I don't know sir."

"Could you try it again?"

"Sir, I ran it through three times."

"Well, could you try once more? Please?"

She took it back with this look that said I was a moron that didn't get it and was holding her up for more important customers. There had to be enough money. I checked my statement two weeks ago and once more three days ago. I had enough to buy three of those necklaces. What was wrong?

As this hag came back to emasculate me in front of the other customers, she put the card down on the glass counter making a loud tack sound reverberating as sweat exploding from my pores and lightness coming over me like water imploding within my flesh dropping to the floor. Embarrassed? Yes. I knew what she was going to say those silly words of apology. Sorry? She wasn't sorry; she wanted to get rid of me in the nicest way possible. She really wanted to tell me to fuck off I need to make a sale. Now the question was do I push her to do it. It would be a battle of niceties, try to be as courteous as possible until one of you cracks and is embarrassed. I was pissed off so much for not knowing how I lost so much money when it wasn't my fault and I thought I might as well take it out on her. So I commenced.

"Well?"

"I'm sorry sir. It still would not go through."

"I don't understand. Ma'am, I know I have money and I just can't understand why it won't." I decided to play it like an unconfident young man to play the sympathy card on the rest of the customers while getting advantage on this witch. My mistake was that it was after Thanksgiving and when people are shopping for loved ones they don't give a damn about anyone else's problem.

"Oh god, come on," I heard someone in the crowd say loud enough for me to hear. But I would not falter.

"Please sir, other customers are waiting," she said while looking at the woman behind me.

"Look, ma'am, maybe you could help me out. I need this necklace. My girlfriend's birthday is coming really close and then there's Christmas right up around the bend. I need this for Christmas cause her birthday gift is already gotten for and I don't want to use her birthday gift for

Christmas and get something stupid for her birthday."

"I'm sorry sir, but I can't help you."

She must've read 'Liar' on my forehead or the huge neon sign behind me saying the same and was actually thinking I'm trying to get this gift for nothing. But I wasn't playing that game. My play was to make this hag really as irritated as I was because of her, so I wanted to be the reason for her irritation.

"But ma'am, you don't understand."

"No sir, I need to take this young woman."

"Wait ma'am, I really need you to try it maybe at least this one more time," as I jumped in front of the next customer face to face with the witch.

"Oh, come on," came from the peanut gallery.

I could see her frustration in her constricting lips creating more wrinkles than there actually were. Her eyes wanted to cut through me but I wouldn't allow her daggers to pierce my armor of this personality I was portraying. I wasn't going to break character.

"Sir, I will try this one more time. Then you will have to go."

"Oh thank you, thank you."

"I'm sorry, sir, no. Now please go," she said as she came back.

"But you don't under…"

"Sir, go away!" She screamed. She broke. I was done.

"Thank you," I Grinch-smiled at her.

I turned around and walked away. I heard the witch and the female customer saying something about me but I didn't care. Walking past the line of ravenous buyers itching to get out of the store, I saw one man sticking out from the rest. He wore a puffy tan grey green mix jacket that made him look twice his size when he was already twice mine. Baggy pants that had seen better days clung to his body out of respect to everyone not wanting to see what he was packing or what would be exploding from behind. A stupid look of idiocy displayed itself to me. Shaggy top, short sides, five o'clock shadow and the open hole he was heavily breathing with looked ridiculous to me.

He gave me his thanks with a 'buddy' at the end and I smiled. Then I saw myself hit him, one straight shot to the face. I'd kicked him down on the floor and sit on his medicine ball of a belly wailing on his sorry excuse of a face. Everyone would gather around us and do nothing because of the fear that would've been installed from my first action. But I didn't do it. I just smiled and told him that he had no idea and walked away.

I stopped by the closest ATM and dipped in my card. The routine of searching for my account ensued and there it was. I saw the zeros like little faces laughing at me like I tilted my bank account and couldn't do anything except feel my heart drop like the dropping of a silver ball in the pinball drain telling me no more plays can be made. There was no one around for me to be an asshole to so instead I ran my hand through my hair grabbing it firmly, sighing, closing my eyes tightly then giving out a scream kicking the wall. Problem was that it was too late for me to ask anyone cause the banks were already closed and having to work during the day I had to wait another week to go and seek someone out.

Next Saturday, I got to the bank early enough to be fourth on line. I don't know how but the elderly are supposed to be slow so that everyone just passes by them and yet there's two old women in front of me and some guy in sweats like he's ready to take his daughter to her elementary basketball practice. But what bothered me was that these two bags of wrinkles just stood at the only two open windows. It was like they were asking for the same thing. I need to count my pennies, I heard one of them say. I think it was the uglier one. Can you count my change young man, the other said. She was the uglier one, maybe. It didn't matter, I couldn't tell from the back. All I remember is that one was hideous and the other looked like a short Bea Arthur. Standing on that line staring into space, staring into the patterns following certain lines moving eclectically, electrically, I could swear that an hour of my life was wasted in twenty minutes and three more went by to finish out the actual hour. But I could see my life pass as each tick of the second hand clicked by passing the twelve making the minute hand whiplash to the next minute in matching with the flicks of Ugly Arthur's pennies tapping onto the beige formica counter top adding up to three freaking dollars and sixteen cents while the change from Short Arthur was dropping on the same top in an unrhythmic pattern contrasting the pennies mathematically creating its own sound of five dollars and fifteen cents as my eyes moved snail speed from the clock to the rug mapping out the Long Island Expy and the Northern and Southern State parkways but finding there was no Meadowbrook, Cross Island or Clearview highways roaming around. Then the Arthurs left. Sweat clothes man went to the left and I went to the right.

"Good morning, how may I help you?"

"I'm having trouble with my account and I'd like to find out what the problem is," I said to the teller.

"Okay, what trouble are you having?"

I explained how I work everyday and I have direct deposit so my money goes straight into my account knowing that there shouldn't be any problems. In telling her this, I fell into the old trap, like everyone else, giving her a story, though true, is still annoying to anyone having to listen to it. Tellers of the story just want listeners to have pity and some feelings to let them get what they want. It didn't work with the hag and the necklace but that wasn't my intention anyway. Here with the bank teller I was trying to get some answers.

"And so I went to an ATM and I saw zeros knowing full well that I have a few thousand dollars and it's driving me nuts on how such a thing could happen. So I was hoping that maybe you could check my account and see if there is any money or check the transactions or something," I spieled searching for that sympathy.

"Well, if you could give me your account number and a photo I. D. I could check it for you."

I said, sure, and handed her my driver's license that was of no use to me since I didn't have a car but I got it anyway. I figured it might eventually come in handy and it has on occasion at work when I have to pick up supplies from a supply house for maintenance purposes using the company pick-up truck. Other than that who really wants an identification card when you could learn to drive if you ever want a car one day. Or use other people's for that matter.

"Well, it says here that you *don't* have money," she said after confirming it on the computer.

"But that can't be."

Then she gave me that look of sorrow.

"Sorry, but that's what the computer says," pointing to the screen knowing that I couldn't see it anyway.

"Could you check what transactions were made?"

"I could make you a print-out."

"That'd be fine."

I heard some tapping of buttons and that clicking of a printer as the cartridges move back and forth writing out what you asked for but not what you want to see. She turned around to the printer that sat behind her and spun back in her chair to hand me the copy. I looked through all the items.

"I didn't make any of these purchases."

"Your name is Dennis Bock and it says you bought those items. Did you lose your card or have it stolen?"

"It's Dennis J. Bock and no, it's right here," as I handed her my plastic means of survival.

"Then I don't know what to say," she said after she looked at my name and expiration date then handed it back. "Hold on one minute. I'm going to ask someone."

She was gone. Not completely, I could see her as she moved from side to side heading to the only floor clerk that was there. He was a puffy gentleman, could tell by the face. And from the white hair you knew he was an older man. I don't know what they were saying but I can imagine it went something like: This guy thinks I'm an idiot, Well what does he want, I don't know maybe he's looking for some cash for me to give him, Did he ask for money, No but that's because he's doing a horrible job, Okay let me talk to him. She nodded and he got up and they walked over.

"Hello there. Why don't you come over to my desk and we can work this out," puffy man said in soprano pitch like Louie Anderson without the annoying raspiness.

Nodding in agreement I walked over with this guy and explained to him everything over again. He too nodded now in trying to comprehend where my trick played on when there was none to be made.

"So what you're telling me is that these items that were purchased under your name, right, were in fact not purchased by you," now he sounded like Jay Leno with the annoyance factor.

"Right."

He pivoted in his chair to the computer and pounded on some keys. After staring at the screen saying that "mm-hmm" sound, the creaks and cracks of his pivoting made me wonder if the chair was alright and sturdy enough to hold him. In one swivel, puffy man told me, one second, and picked up the phone and dialed. I can tell he's done this before with the swiftness and grace he possessed in calling whoever it was but no matter how many times he'd done it that swivel chair was not used to it. Then he said, okay, and hung up.

"Well son, it appears that the items were purchased in Canada."

"Canada?"

"Canada."

I don't remember ever taking a trip to Canada and I told him so.

"Not ever?" he asked.

"No, but not recently."

I had been there a long time ago as a kid with my parents but that had nothing to do with now. Now I was this adult with a job, no time for random traveling, got to work all day everyday to make the all-American dollar.

"You know, it's quite possible that someone had taken a picture of your card with one of those camera phones and used it in Canada or sold it to someone in Canada."

It sounded convincing enough, I thought. It just got me upset. When I didn't know what happened rage was my friend burning inside wanting out on anyone; once there's an explanation given or some understanding the volume of rage and anger seems to turn down because now you know the answer. Your flames turn to a kindle of depression and being upset. Even though it wasn't *the* answer, it was *an* answer.

The upcoming Monday I went to the payroll department at work and had them change my direct deposit to giving me a check every week. Why, asked the lady behind the desk. I told her that my account at the bank was having issues. Nobody really needs to know my business, not entirely. But after that was all sorted, I began cashing my checks, waiting on line the length of a soup kitchen line for everyone and their mother heading to the bank. I wouldn't even dare go to one of those check cashing spots, the lines there are like waiting to see Santa. I'd rather wait on the soup kitchen line than on a Santa line, at the end at least you know you're getting something real. With that aside, my cash would then be brought home and put in an envelope and kept in my drawer underneath socks but it'd be under my mattress when I went to bed.

Soon enough Christmas rolled around. Tree, presents,

family, loved ones, the whole shebang. The only oddity was that snow had not shown up. Mild front from the south pushing north is how the weatherman put it. Seeing the red arrows moving up along the East Coast, he's showing viewers what its like throughout the nation.

"Come on, Dennis, put the TV on *A Christmas Carol?*" my brother said entering in the living room. "Nobody wants to watch the news."

"Its not the news; it's the weather."

"So."

"Fine."

I switched channels over to the station that was playing Dickens all day. I think they showed every version of *A Christmas Carol* from Patrick Stewart to the old black and white unknown actors. Flipping channels again, finding another station that was also playing Dickens. Then it was like clockwork with each, *It's a Wonderful Life*, *A Christmas Story*, clay-mation Rudolph and Santa, animation Rudolph and Santa. It would never end.

"It never ends," as I sought salvation from the ceiling with open palms. "Why God, why?"

"Oh stop," Shusha came in saying from getting me a drink. "You whine too much," jokingly. Then she handed me our drinks and settled herself next to me. Taking off her shoes first, then knees on the couch and her ass went down to her ankles. I had lifted up my arm so she could nestle into me and she took her glass as my arm came down gently onto her body. Her hands combed through my hair. "Finally you cut your hair. Good." I said nothing. She had asked me repeatedly to get a haircut but I had repeatedly refused. I figured since I couldn't get the necklace I should double up on gifts. She was like this lump of love attached to me, not like a tumor, but rather a mole or blood pimple that's always been there and you've grown accustomed to it once you really notice it every time you look in the mirror.

As the rest of my family congregated around the television/Christmas tree (they were next to each other, but some eyes were on the screen while others concentrated on the season), my mind was a bit restless on the gift I had gotten for Shusha. Knowing that it was not even my second choice but rather what I could afford for her bothered me and I know that this stupid holiday is not about what you're giving but rather that it's actually the fact that you thought of that person, well, bullshit. It's in the eyes of those children when they open up a box revealing a pair of socks or a sweater; the mouth that says thank you and makes attempts at cracking a smile, but the eyes come to the first realization of disappointment. Granted there are other presents there, but only to balance out this horrible effect. And as one gets older, those toys seem to disappear to time and only surviving in memory where phrases like "Oh wow, I remember this G. I. Joe" and "This takes me back" and finally coming to adulthood where you're even lucky if you get a gift and then supposed to look thankful. Yet there's always that one gift that someone gives you, whether its your mother, brother, cousin, girlfriend, boyfriend, it doesn't matter who, but it hits you and triggers that memory to give the sensation that the Barbie Doll or Teenage Mutant Ninja Turtle used to and that dolphin necklace was it. And I couldn't give it to her.

The aroma of gingerbread lingered in the air as presents were handed out, torn wrapping paper crunched and crackled on the floor and "ooo's" and "aah's" died out so everyone could leave. Once the house was quiet, Shusha and I were alone. My mom and brother had gone to bed. Shusha grabbed my hand and I followed her to my room. We had decided to give each other presents after everyone else had gone home. Was I expecting that magical gift from her? No, not really. But through her excitement and smiles, I could tell she believed she had. So how does one actually give off that sensation without giving it away in your eyes? You don't let them look at your eyes.

"Oh wow," as I kept looking down. She was waiting to see my face. I didn't want to give her that taste. I knew she'd sense the disappointment from lack of excitement and it'd be like poison buried inside, only growing to spring up on me when the time's right.

"You don't like it." She didn't sound pouty or annoyed. It was more a bland response. It came out of nowhere.

"What do you mean, I love it."

"You won't look at me. I even got it with your name on it."

I forgot about the "not-looking" part. You can't look at them but you can't not look at them either. You're damned either way. It's the inevitability of the season. You know you're getting presents so you know you're getting disappointment. Like Halloween or Thanksgiving, you know you're eating too much and something bad's coming out of your ass.

"I like it. I can use it." The old 'I can use it' bit. It's supposed to mean it's a good buy. Honestly, how many fucking journals can one guy have? Personally I like buying my own. Journals are a personal thing. The journal fits into you, you don't fit into the journal. One stares at every single empty book that waits to be written in. But the one calling out to you, whether through style, color, or a word, that's the one you chose. It doesn't help that she had it personalized. Anyway, I knew what was coming. I handed her the little box I had kept on to. Don't get any ideas; proposing was the last thing on my mind.

"I don't like it."

Please. What woman doesn't like jewelry? It wasn't the dolphins but good enough.

"But I can use it," she added.

I could tell she was upset, no kidding, right. But I had to skip a couple of payments to get it and I don't think she should've been that upset, but I wasn't going to tell her that. So I knew this night wasn't going to have a happy ending. She was going to go and not talk to me for a few days. To cool off mostly. She wasn't upset about the gift, I don't think. It was more of the effort that she went into getting it engraved with my name. I would have asked her why my middle name or initial wasn't there but that'd only make her more irritated.

After she had calmed down, she called me a couple of days later and asked what were our plans for New Year's. I told her I had no idea and asked if she was mad at me. She replied in the affirmative and said she was getting over it little by little. She also had added that 'Just cause I'm mad doesn't mean we can't spend holidays together. You can make it up to me.'

"Okay. I'll call you when I've made plans."

"Okay."

And she hung up. Didn't see her until New Year's Eve

and she asked what we were up to. I had wanted to go into the city to see the ball drop. I'd never done it so I thought it was time to journey out into the unknown. She couldn't see why but she agreed to it as there was nothing else. From the corner of my eye, the earrings I got her for Christmas hung from her lobes blatantly showing off that she liked my gift but shoving in my face that I hadn't used her present at all. She didn't know that but I waited for the question.

"So have you written anything lately?" as she stared out of the train into the sunset horizon of Queens.

As a writer, for me anyway, that's a kind of question you hate getting asked. It's like asking a musician if he's practiced at all. Of course I've been writing but there are days when you don't do it in the physical sense cause it's being worked on in your brain. It won't be perfect from your head, of course, trying to perfect something in the giant nerve of a brain is stupidity. But what's going on is the laying of some ground work so that when you do get it on paper its close to what you want. Then edit around your framework. Every discipline has a quirk surrounding it, not everyone works the same.

"I've been doing something but it's not coming out right to put it on paper," was my response. All she said was, Oh, and that was it. "I have been writing in the book though." She gave me no response. But I did write in it. I was working a couple of stories, making notes and everything. But I don't think she wanted to hear it.

I held her all along the way, through the tunnels of the city but she was nowhere near me. The eyes pointed out the glass to the escape where she was. I didn't question her on it; my mind was focused on other things as well.

All my money sitting underneath underwear this time cause I changed it from socks thinking my brother would go through it maybe looking for a little cash. Would he, I don't know. Hard to say. It was just a precaution. I still wanted to know how someone could have gotten my number and bought things in Canada. Unless he, or she, was a crafty Canadian coming to con credulous counterparts. But that's ridiculous. Anything could be possible and I was looking for an answer to which there were hundreds.

Coming out of the subway, traffic was directed to walk towards Central Park and passing by block after block, roads had been closed with an officer standing guard making sure nobody got in through a side entrance. You could see the sea of heads a touch faster than normal only to be closer to see the sight than having to watch a blip of light move an inch. There we were, caught in the middle like cattle stuffed through narrow steel gates to officers patting us down rushing once again to be ahead of the pack crowded together by more steel gates.

Making it to the back of a packed street, I could see the thousands of people that had come to see this annual event. My memory of every New Year's that I could recall from the time I was young enough to comprehend what it was passed like a slideshow progressively losing its allure and importance in hopes that this time, this journey, would bring back some grandeur. For some reason *Forrest Gump* popped in my head. That scene where Gump and Lt. Dan are in the bar celebrating and once the ball drops, Lt. Dan has an empty look framed by debauchery emitting from the screen. Gump is too dumb to understand and all the celebrants are too eager to drink themselves stupid to realize, but Lt. Dan knew. He knew that loss and that's why I came. To see if I can find that childlike excitement for this holiday. War ruined him; time ruined me. You could hear the joy coming from Times Square. But back where we were, conversations about personal lives filled my ears.

Standing and waiting, people pushed forward to try and get as close as they could. Friends finding each other brought food to loved ones. People hung out of open windows tossing locks of toilet paper to us below. The bright lights of Times Square reached only so far to get to the darkness that held late comers. The size of the edifices viced us together adding to the blockage of light.

"What time is it?" I heard someone say. Then came the voices all around me in stereo. It's almost time, I think its eleven fifty, The ball already dropped, How can you tell, Its three minutes to twelve, Well I got two minutes, But I checked the weather channel, The ball doesn't move until a minute before, I thought it was two minutes.

"Look its eleven fifty-nine. The ball's moving," someone pointed out with his binoculars.

As tiny as the ball was, it was moving. In my mental deliberation of youth and cinematic analysis, I had forgotten that this was the moment for preparation. My arms found themselves sliding around Shusha congealing with the curvature of her waist while heat soldered us together. Her cold hands pressed upon mine to warm up. My head rested on hers only slightly so as not to put too much pressure. Our eyes fixed on the small light and heard out of our ears someone saying that it was almost time.

Screams of the upcoming New Year landed heavily in my ears. Arms flailing about waving streamers and signs.

I looked at my watch in anticipation but unfortunately my watch was already in the New Year, about three and a half minutes into it. I turned my attention back to the ball then I questioned myself if I remembered the words to Auld Lang Syne. I thought it was stupid for anyone to actually know the words, maybe a couple of lines but not the whole thing. It's not really an important song, just something to say. What the hell does Auld Lang Syne mean anyway?

"Alright everybody."

I kept quiet while everybody else was chanting along.

"Ten."

"Nine."

"Eight." I squeezed Shusha's hand.

"Seven."

"Six."

"Five." I turned Shusha around.

"Four."

"Three."

"Two." Our eyes met.

"One…"

JANUARY

"…Happy New Year!" There's that moment between time and days when its magic milliseconds passing on by. It's those moments in movies where silence takes up all the space around you and twinkles in eyes are seen. I like to think we shared that moment as we kissed. Saliva passed between us; our arms encircled each other. Eternity lingered for only a millisecond from one year to the next. Though I smiled at her I knew there was nothing. I was still playing the game, the charade that cast its shadow upon me many years ago. Lt. Dan would be upset for my playing along, but I believe he found religion or God which smells of hypocrisy. I don't think I'll be that lucky.

"Its nice being here," Shusha said within the roar of the crowd.

Sentimentality. It's something that's used in stories to get to the emotions of the voyeur. You cry at the scenes of the hero or a loved one dying. Even at the moments where the hero triumphs over tribulation, you get that warm fuzzy feeling inside. I put up with hers because I love her. And love, as what some people say, is about giving and taking in the relationship, compromise. But I think it's mostly just being able to put up with the other person's bullshit.

"Yeah, babe, it's nice."

We didn't last too long after that. Her Delilah beauty must have been too much for my unlikeness to Victor Mature. She needed something more than what I was giving her so with the new year, new changes needed to be made. Even if that change meant going back to something that previously seemed ill but after some time now was right after all.

almost a year ago

Shifting in my chair from watching an almost three hour flick, the pain lifted me up and out of the theater that I went outside into that January chill to stretch my legs. My feet pounded themselves on the cement step to revive the numbness in my ass while, coincidently, keeping me warm. Killing two birds with one stone. Looking through the glass door, a line of people were waiting on line for tickets. Groups of friends laughing it up at stupidity that someone said and couples holding hands or kissing. The bright hooker red of the columns and matching door frame surrounded me like cold flames of Hell keeping guard over me so that escape was not an option.

Also keeping sentry, witness to my wackiness, a sienna girl with long black hair wearing a long blue overcoat with red eyes happened to be sitting to my right on a stone, no no, it was a wooden bench. Her ethereal reflection was caught in the glass and realizing she was there, I turned to see that her ghostly form had become solid. The redness in her eyes meant sadness, crying. And it sparked my interest.

"Cold night, huh?" I questioned as I stepped over. I could tell she didn't hear the question. "Hello? Are you okay?"

"What? Huh? Oh…yes. I'm fine."

"Yeah well, you don't look it."

"Oh, I know." She laughed a little. "I'm a bit of a wreck."

"No, not really. More like a fender bender."

I don't think she got the joke but she sort of did this giggle laugh that girls do after they've been crying. Maybe she did get it. After a short silence, we got to talking about her friends dragging her out when she didn't want to. I sympathized with I'm not much of a "going to the movies" guy but my friends also took me out to see some WWII movie and adding that sitting through a movie and previews for over two and a half hours…

"…is not really fun on your bum, if you know what I mean," as I made a coy smile at the thought of using the word "bum". Didn't want to be too rude upon meeting a pretty girl, but she did laugh so I knew I was okay. "Cold night though. I'm wondering when this snow's gonna melt. I'm ready for summer."

"Yeah." A distance suddenly appeared by my silly statement. I had to recover.

"You have very pretty eyes, even if you had been crying."

She smiled again which told me that she was in. I pointed to the seat and she said 'yeah, sure' as she turned towards me. I sat on that cold stone, it wasn't wooden it was stone, bench and gave her that look of interest. I took a quick look at my watch and then into her eyes.

"My friends will probably be coming out soon looking for me or maybe your friends will come out and end this unexpected meeting but I was wondering maybe I could get your name and number. I could give you a call and we can have a warmer conversation." Then came the cheesy line. "Maybe stop the world and melt some of this snow with you?"

"My name is Shusha," she said. Then she held out her hand and I kissed it.

"A princess' hand should be kissed."

We talked about her Armenian-Azerbaijani history with her name and my intrigue into who she was. But then as my friends serendipitously walked out, she remarked that she was crazy but exchanged phone numbers. I told her that I had to go cause they were my ride but that I'd keep in touch. As if it was fate I was hoping this relationship would last but never meet a girl in January, it would begin as it would end.

A couple of weeks after we went to see the ball drop she dropped a ball on me. I didn't think that there was anything wrong when I first met her except that she was hiding something which drew me to her in the beginning. Didn't know it would bite me in the ass. She came to see me and said we needed to talk. "Needing to talk" is never a good sign.

She sat me down and she began discussing how we met and asked if I remembered. I told her, 'Yeah, the Germans were wearing grey and you wore blue'. She mentioned she wasn't over her boyfriend who had just broken up with her. She was always mopey and after a few days her friends took her out and that's when we met. But now the ex was back. She didn't weigh anything, there was no see-sawing, she just said...

"I still have feelings for him and you were just there to keep him off my mind. I did like you and it was fun, but you whine too much." This time it wasn't a joke. She had turned that heartbeat over again for him as it had once beat for me. Shusha told me that when she heard Van Morrison's "Astral Weeks" a realization of her affections for her ex were not yet over but needed to be born again by their separation. Which to me was bullshit considering I gave her that album when she only knew "Brown-Eyed Girl" and I wanted to expand her musical taste and knowledge.

I began with the usual "oh my god" and "I can't believe this". If I said I didn't want to cry that'd be a lie. Not cry so much as tear up. I felt the urge, but to keep my manly status I held back. But when she said that they had been seeing each other for the past couple of weeks, not officially (whatever that means), she found that she cared for him; I told her that she wasn't that attractive anyway with a narrow nose and chunky cheeks and stagnant Botox face, which is what I think Swann should have told Odette instead of just walking away. Bitch. Then she was out of my life and still kept the Christmas present. And I, alone once again for the oncoming of February.

2

I got up from my bed to get a closer look at the mole on the wall. My brother, while continuing his IM's, asked me what I was doing. I told him about the dark mark on my white walls. He turned to look and said it must be a shadow. But I eyed the ceiling and knew there was nothing obstructing the light's rays. I licked my fingers and tried rubbing it off but nothing happened. Then he added that nothing in this world is perfect as much as we try to make it be.

"The only perfection is imperfection," I said. While still staring at the computer screen, he agreed.

Gazing at my brother's melon, imagining the hair that once was there now lost, drove a question inside of me that had to be expunged verbally and so I asked him why he shaved his head. Then, rotating to me once more, he looked me in the eyes. In these eyes came the memory I wished to forget. In these eyes sent that cold cruel jingle shiver down my spine; it was the eyes I'd seen once before that now reminded me of my guilt. He didn't have to ask *the* question but he asked a different question that told me he knew something.

"You tell me why you 'quit' your job," as he threw up the air quotes with his fingers. "And I'll tell you why I shaved my head?"

I had to think fast because he knew I'd be lying if I waited too long. Stalling with the usual sibling refrains of "you first" and "I asked you first" gave me a little time to get my ideas in order. Giving him only the partial truth, I told him the tale that the job really wasn't cutting it for me as a writer. I needed to go out and see things, experience life as they say, and work on my craft. I told him the trip I took was a journey to see something new and cleanse myself of that life to enter the new phase "pure". I wondered if that would be enough for him to give me what I wanted and not tell him the whole truth.

"Is that why you painted your room white? To start with a clean slate?"

"Yes," I told him so he could go on and tell me his story.

"Too bad you're heading into that new phase with a blotch on your record."

Jokingly he said this but I didn't see it as a joke. Either he knew or he could read my face, I couldn't tell which. It was then I knew it would eat away at my mind, my soul unless I did something about it. But what? And so I thought as he told me some story about breaking up with his girlfriend and it hit him hard. I guess it was going to somewhat parallel to me but I wasn't paying attention anymore. I remembered Raskolnikov and his secretive nature and eventual confession of the secret that grew inside him waiting to burst out. It takes a strong will to not want to tell what's behind the eyes once it begins to gnaw on the brain.

I excused myself from my brother and headed down to the basement. Dark and cold with the humidifier humming to get rid of moisture, I went over to my desk with my notebooks overflowing on top flipping open the first one I saw. I switched on the lamp brightening one corner of the room and sat prolifically before the magnificent open page. It was blank, like a silence on a Sunday morning funeral, nothing written and I was about to bury the casket and sign the tombstone. I became a recording instrument and this acknowledgement of what had passed in my life now was in front of my senses to be written. Never to be read by anyone but out of my system that it should never haunt me ever, I wrote my confession.

FEBRUARY

Getting over Shusha was partly simple and complex at the same time. I couldn't just forget about her due to the burn being too recent so it was still stuck in my head. All the things we did that couples do; going out, eating together, music we shared, discussing whatever topic happened to appear. All these memories were still lodged within brain cells, still fresh. My missing CD's that I leant her; holes in my collection were a missing part of me. Gifts that she'd given me lying around reminding me of her and I couldn't just give or throw away.

Time, I knew, would close this wound so my only option to get through this was to throw myself into work; to think about something else is the only way to get rid of what's on your mind. And it works. I began thinking of ways to clean the bathroom quicker or at least make it cleaner using a different style of soap solution. I had figured out the best pathway through the factory so I wouldn't have to return to the same spot repeatedly. In trying to save my company money, when hand soap lotion levels were low I'd change the cartridge and save all the leftover lotion and use it as a floor cleaner. Sometimes I even made sure the workers didn't take too much paper to dry their hands after washing. They found this annoying so I made a sign over every towel dispenser in big black letters informing them to take only two towels and no more. I remember that was also the time I made a sign to use the garbage can as a disposal for paper waste, not the floor or the toilet. And then a third sign as a reminder that the floor nor the sink was a toilet.

"Whaat zah 'ell is zahmatta wiz you?" Remy asked as he came over to talk to me. He was borderline forty heading into thirty, only a few inches taller than me and the white rose out of his peppered hair as it mixed with the black. He had the girth of an overachieving sapling while his attitude reverberated of a Judas Priest song and like most Frenchmen hated American politics but he himself fell in love with American music and literature. It was only twelve years ago that he had come over from the town of Brest. When I asked about his home his reply was..."We are zuh suppell neepull of F'ance, firm and gzenteel." One time he told me that as a boy he would reach the point and look out over the Atlantic wishing one day to come to America. When I asked why he wanted to come to America so badly, his response was he wanted a Milleresque experience but he'd rather it be New York than Paris.

"Why duex you make it so 'ard for yourself? You make it fucking 'ard for me too," he continued on. Remy was the night porter when I was hired for the day shift. He preferred working at night, said it fit in with his lifestyle. He didn't like crowds. And walking around during the day was out, so sleep was in order. He began work after I got off which was around threeish. Thus began his eight hour shift of sweeping, mopping, vacuuming, cleaning anything that needed to be done and finishing around eleven. After, he would begin his living after midnight. Trips to 24 hour stores to purchase necessities for the house like bread, milk, and frozen dinners ready to be nuked in the microwave. If such trips were not needed then the bars would be his aim in search of fun and pleasure. Everything else that had to be dealt with during the day was taken care of through the mail. "To live durring zuh day you 'ave to deal wiz people prretending fo' sum sush rreason. At night, we become oo we want to be," he told me once. After we first met, he came early to sit and chat with me everyday about what was going in our lives, in the company, in the world. We'd listen to the radio, changing it from music to talk shows depending on mood. But all we'd share together was one hour, experiencing each other for that moment over a long period of time. It was enough for us to get along.

I told him how I was trying to get over Shusha leaving me. "Oh pleeze. Wemen." I listened as he explained to me the differences between men and women. Men, he said, are creators, inventors, the want for something new while women are destroyers, they tear things down. When I asked him wasn't it the other way around, he said it wasn't. Men hide behind the veil of security to appear as destroyers, to seem tough amongst each other and women, but men are truly weak inside. Women, he added, are the opposite, behind the veil of weakness they are truly strong and only reveal themselves when domination of a man is complete.

"Empyres fell; waars were fought because of wemen."

"But why then do we need them?" I inquired.

"Zat is zuh crool trick of Gud, oo to me is a woman. We plant zuh seed to grrow and zay burce zuh fruit zat dyes. We sink immortality, zay see finality. Zat is why I understand my fahzah when 'e tol' me zat zer a' two sings in life. Won, get as much pussy as you can. An' two, don' 'ave children. And I 'ave done botz."

Though I don't think I understood, I didn't pursue in questioning. He asked me why Shusha left and I gave him the reason why but he told me it was garbage.

" 'Ave you ever used your tongue?"

"What?"

"You probably didin' lick her."

"*Like* her?"

"No, LICK, LICK HER."

"What does that have to do with it?"

"Ah, show me a man oo doesn't lick pussy, and I will make 'er a 'appy wife."

As I got up to go, Remy told me not to worry about it and that there are plenty more holes to punch. I reminded him that I knew but this was just so sudden with Valentine's Day quickly approaching it would be a while before I got over her. Not like him whose relationships last for a few hours. Then I walked away overhearing the disc jockey, "Wow another warm day done and one more to come. This winter has been bright and sunny. I'll tell ya folks, we've been spoiled. But you know what that means, don't ya? Yes, yes a cold spring is a-comin', so start getting prepared for a spring frost but don't worry about it right now cause Valentine's Day is around the corner. So warm up next to your sweetheart as we listen to 'Feels Like The First Time'." To me, I was feeling cold as ice.

Staring. Out into empty space in front of me, just staring. Behind the emptiness were the floor and sky and sandwiched in between was the life in progress. But I concentrated on the space. My eyes would occasionally avert themselves to couples holding hands or kissing or feeding each other. And how I despised them for their happiness.

Valentine's Day. The illusory holiday. A month is not enough time for a guy to really screw up. Consider this, a guy does some dumb things. Come Christmas, you forgive him but not really. New Year's rolls around and you both get a fresh start, clean slate. Then comes Valentine's Day and there's no data for what's going on so the assumption of all's well sets in and there's the illusion.

But just as a magician creates an illusion, if the assistant doesn't come through in the end then the illusion is lost, setting up for something later. The assistant in the relationship is the male. Like the time I saw this woman crying and from overhearing the conversation the guy forgot she was allergic to blossoms, didn't like the color lavender and for strike three, she was a vegetarian. I could only guess that they'd gone out for a while and expectance to know intricacies was important.

Emotionally, I was all mixed up. Like an onion has layers, these were mine, in no particular order. Part of me was hurt, singing its rendition of "There Goes My Baby". Scarred and torn up inside, memories of our time together, the happy moments that were oh so darling, kept coming back to me. Another side of myself was paying attention to Zappa's "Go Cry On Someone Else's Shoulder". Pissed as I was, what did she really mean to me? Like a slide show right along with those darling slides flashed the arguments, the headaches, and the lies. Curled fists hoped for destruction. My libido, insecure, hid in the corner of my mind. Questioning myself as if I were good enough sexually, the tears lulled behind my eyes never once escaping but ready to weep at my own inability to satisfy. Then again, images of her moaning my name and performing fellatio found its way in my mind's projector. Trapped by this wallow, I stared in a daze, moving nowhere because my mind was pulling in different directions, and waited for the day at least to pass before this shit-filled thought process could end.

And like an onion sitting out in the sun, I began to reek. I would have to say the rotting away began at this bright and sunny not-a-good-idea-to-go-to-the-park day. The aroma of unwashed flesh rose from my pores and crevices reaching only so high and then sticking around. Sunlight gave invisibility to this smell as it slithered and swirled but looking closely, the haze it created encircled me.

In the wide world of singles, you really don't want to be alone. Meaning you don't want to go out into the world alone though many people walking around are single. There are the losers, the weirdoes, the pervs, the uglies, the bad habits, and many other disgusting monikers. When alone, deciding where you fit is where it's hard to figure out. Then there are those people who walk around alone but are really with someone, which happens. But singles tend to hover around couples in some way to be privileged to receive that magic of finding that someone through diffusion.

To break away from the wallow, I met up with my friends the next day, after showering of course. It was the usual garbage of getting together to do nothing. Sitting around uselessly on the couch of David's living room just to drink beer and discuss the ever-present situation of sitting on the couch and drinking beer. David's couch was a bit uncomfortable with the solidity it gained from its continual usage. The dimness of the room I don't think helped much either with the couch. With the curtains slightly letting in light, the couch never really caught the essence of the sun to rejuvenate itself. You couldn't even tell the color of the walls whether they were white, beige, cream or tan. It looked like all of them with the tints of shade varied around the room. But I sat there with them, between David and Mike. And Jeff next to Mike. In front of us was David's entertainment system. A 24" screen television with a stereo system to add more sound so that if the neighbors complained for any reason we wouldn't be able to hear them. It wouldn't be great for the cops to come, but it's never gotten to that point.

"So what are we doing guys?" I asked after taking another swig of beer.

"What do you mean?" said Mike from my left.

"We're watching *Naked Lunch* and drinking some beers," David threw in from my right. "I just gotta check the scores." He pulled out his cell as if looking for answers to mystical questions.

"But all we do is fucking drink beer and watch movies."

"Yeah, but wasn't it you who said that we're all gonna die, and that is our eventual end so we should enjoy ourselves while we can. Wasn't that in some story you were writing? What happened to that story?" returned Mike.

"Never got around to finishing it," I said.

"Why not? If you're going to make a drive, you might as well make it to the end zone," David commentated while putting away his cell.

"I can't find the time," I lied as I could see Robocop without his armor talking to a bug of a typewriter of some anti-terrorism action squad. There was time; I just chose not to find it.

"So what do you want to do?" Jeff piped in from the far left.

"I don't know. Something."

"Hey David, go get the bong. This movie will really bug us out then."

Jeff and David laughed at Mike's pun but I wasn't interested in smoking up but now there was no choice. Not that I cared either way. I've toked before but I just didn't want to. David left for a minute to get his ceramic bong in the figure of a fountain trophied it back.

"Don't worry Dennis. This will help you to forget about Sheena or Shiva," Mike said handing over a bud to David.

"Shusha," I corrected.

"Yeah, her. Well, this'll be just like a Dr. Phil session without having to hear his voice." We laughed.

"So, who will have the honor of the first hit?"

"Ah, David, if you don't mind, let's allowDennis here take the first."

"No, it's alright Mike."

"Okay then I will," Jeff came in. "This movie's getting interesting and I need to get more into it."

So David handed over the bong to Jeff along with a

lighter. Jeff tried to keep his eyes on the movie while igniting the bud. Mike turned to David to ask him if the water was good. David said it was so good you could drink it. Jeff made a hand-off to Mike who took his hit. And as I grabbed this imitation of a fountain, representing life in some way, I began thinking. You know when the mind wanders for a bit deducing your life and in traveling never reaches a point but just a pause in thought. Well, my mind was in thought of Shusha still and going over my life and smoking up was going to create a bigger pause than necessary cause I needed to figure out why she left me and why money was disappearing and why did everything now change for me. So I lit that bud and inhaled. My worries and anxieties were still there but at bay; the intoxication stood sentry against them.

Soon enough my mind was a drift in space and time moving at a pace all its own. Now though everything moved while I was seated on the couch making no movements of my muscles. All stationary, immobile objects had gained control of unknown forces within themselves to produce this kinetic energy, forcing mobility, to achieve some concealed purpose hidden from thought. Like waking up in the morning to get ready for work. In that moment you don't know why you're getting up but in the subconscious you know you need the money. Those unknown forces, what we never really notice, are our bodies telling us we must move in order to keep ourselves alive. The very cells we learn about in elementary school that are in constant work mode binding together for the simple task of their own survival create the community for you to keep on surviving as well. And the cell has its own life process much like an animal of beginning, living then dying only to perpetuate whatever this happens to be; also much like an atom where it just is in being what it is. The atom or cell knows not what it does. It doesn't even *know*; it just is. Life is that concealed purpose few people ever think about, imagining some divine riddle that needs to be answered but in fact its answerable if stopped. To look and see how we fit into the "plan of Life" and not how Life fits into ours. But I was lost in how walls transformed into trees and the couch diluted into nothing, but the comfort was still attached to me while the television screen expanded swallowing us inside, that we were starring in our own show that revolved around us. It was then I knew the theme song of that moment where we were standing around dangling in silence and I being self-appointed music composer of the show switched on the song.

"I don't believe in magic," I began mumbling to myself only to get progressively louder. "I don't believe in tarot." Gradually the others joined in also until I said my last line. "I just believe in me." But while they continued on, I stared into a pond that suddenly appeared showing me a reflection of my unconscious self. This is what I look like inside, I thought; there was no faith. And, to me, nothing could be done about it.

After a couple of days of feeling sorry for myself, I got back to work making sure toilets were spotless but laying off the obsessiveness. Didn't need employees hounding me about why they should care what I do and asking if they can help out. At this point, if it's dirty and needs a clean, that's job security. Other employees had to worry about their own machines, not check to see if they aimed right at the toilet, floor or wall.

"You know whaat you need," Remy came up to me one day. "A gud fuck." He proceeded to inform me that there is a special cunt out there that makes you feel like you're in a warm cozy bed. I think he was quoting Miller to me in paraphrase but I let him continue.

He told me this type of female was very rare and hard to find. I scoffed in laughter but he said that this specialty could be in any woman. Whether she was a whore, a bitch, an angel, a virgin made no difference. He said he only found it twice in his life. The first was with this French prostitute around Montemarte while he stayed in Paris for a few months. Her name was Michelle but to Remy, she was Michy. She took care of herself with her douche and shower but the apartment was a mess minus the bed. He met her in some bar talking up some tourist from America and he was offended that their French girls wouldn't want French men so he went over and stole her away. The aroma, the heat coming from between her legs elevated to his nostrils as he stood above her. And then all he could remember was feeling his entire body being surrounded. It was as if Michy had metamorphosed into a human sized cunt and he had to use his entire body to do it justice. He said he laid down right inside, cheek to clitoris, massaging her with his face. But he knew it wouldn't be enough so he used his tongue, his hands, his legs, his feet. He was swimming in that warm, fleshy bed. And when it was over realizing he had to pay, he knew she was the best lay around. He went back many more times after that first one, he said. But being the best has its consequences. After Remy came to America, he found out years later that she died because of two things. One, with such a wonderful gift there's bound to be a jealous man who doesn't want there to be any others. The guy who shot her and a customer in mid-coital was arrested for double homicide and pled insanity where he now sits in an insane asylum. Two, during the autopsy doctors found she had AIDS from screwing so many guys but she never checked herself probably thinking her douche worked wonders. The guy in the asylum got it too. So, in turn, she got her revenge.

"Naturally, I whent an got masef tested zjust to be saf. But I criied never sinking I wuld ever 'ave anuzer cunde like zat."

But then, he told me, there was Agnes. She was this businesswoman that he had met one night while strolling around the city. The first thing that he spotted was her widely shaped, slightly curved ass. The way he explained it was she looked like Mary Travers but sounded a lot like Nico. He followed her for a short while and right as she was about to call a cab, he did it for her. Being a gentleman he offered it up but knowing she would refuse, being an independent woman, he offered to split it if they were heading in the same direction. They ended up going to Greenwich which was out of his way, but in the cab they talked. He told her his life minus sexual exploits; she said she came over from Poland a few years ago, working in some firm, making boo-coo bucks, and even mentioning a boyfriend. Remy returned with a smirk and a reply of that the boyfriend had nothing to do with this conversation. He knew of the Eastern European cold demeanor that a lot of those women obtain growing up and that he wouldn't sleep with her that first night but he did get her number. Two weeks, Remy said, it took him to get her into bed. Then he thought it was about persistence and wearing her down but it was actually she who was running the show.

After he had just about given up, she let it happen. They had gone out to eat fancy which she paid for naturally, only to show her independence. Upon entering her place she let him take charge in undressing her, massaging her nice not big but not small plump tits with nipples coming to a point like daggers, placing his hands on the ass he so wanted and then inserting himself. At that moment, every recollection of Michy came rushing back. Every muscle spasm, every aroma, the feel of the vaginal lining within his muscle memory, senses memory, dick memory was revived even though it had to change with the aura of a different female, boiled down it was the same damn talent.

Relieved he was to find another that was just like Michy. She had been dead for awhile and almost completely forgot about her, but through Agnes he found heaven once more. It was a resurrection that was not to last. Michy had given her gift freely to any comers at a price. To Remy, Michy should've been sanctified in life, San Michy, Our Lady of Everybody, as well as in her death. Amen.

Was it possible that Agnes didn't comprehend the power she possessed with this talent? But once Remy was done, he noticed her leer in the mirror at him and he knew that she did know and would've used it for her own purpose. He ascertained that he would never have it again but she would hold it over him as a bargaining chip, as a Holy Grail beheld but lost forever.

"So eye lef, leeving it be-ind me. Nevur to see 'er agin," Remy finished.

"That's depressing. I would feel worse after that.

Knowing I had the best sex ever and then never having it
again."

"Zer is a difurance between a gud fuck an' za bes' cunt
evur. Won, you can 'ave wiz jus' anywon.... Ze ozer, well,
can only 'appen wiz ze gurl oo 'as it."

"So why did you tell me those stories?" I stared at
Remy hoping he would give me an answer to this heartache.
But from him there were never any answers, just ideas
dressed up made to appear as answers.

"It waz jus' to tell you uv my memoree uv za greytest
sex eye evur 'ad. Eye guess its allso to tell you zat wen
you find zat special won, nevur let it go."

To me, there was no purpose in him telling me his story
except to distract me of what I was feeling inside. For
some guys handling rejection is strange when you've been
with someone and then they don't want you. Its different
if they reject you from the get go cause you can just chalk
it up to looks or speech but if a girl goes with you for
awhile, there's something wrong with you that she thought
she could change for the better. The pit of my stomach felt
that, the rejection. Regardless of how long it's been since
she dumped me, nausea still swam in my intestines. Remy
looked out to the sky without an expression on his face.
He knew what he was leaving and it didn't matter. It was
a fact of life to just move on. It was something I needed
to learn to accept.

"But I guess it coold be zat ze moral iz gud sings cum
an' zen go no matter what."

I didn't like it; I don't think any one person enjoys that
rejection. I had to grow up from that. No man really wants
to grow up. It means to stop acting like a kid, putting away

childish things, accept more responsibility. I thought I had that control of being an adult but I guess I was wrong. I was a writer after all, growing up didn't really fit. In the Bible, it was written that Jesus said for us to be child-like when having faith in God. God has nothing to do with our life on this planet because God comes to everyone differently and for some of us God doesn't exist. But if Jesus meant that we have to be child-like in believing in something greater than ourselves, then sure, I'd be the child and writing is the thing that's bigger than us. I wasn't going to give that up. Rejection, though, is a fact of life also, as is everything else that affects us in anyway. Even the things that have nothing to do with you find a way to get to you. Was I going to search for Shusha? No, it was over. Move on. Next trip. But I couldn't cleanse myself of her because she was the longest relationship I ever had and it was going to be some time. I just didn't know how long. But Mardi Gras was around the corner and after that would be Lent where most Catholics believe that you have to give something up for your faith as a fasting for the oncoming Easter where Jesus died for our sins. And for the Jews it would be Passover which Jesus celebrated. Maybe I could purge her from my mind.

My friends and I reunited at this bar called Tammy O'Sheen's and it was all decked out with Mardi Gras apparel. Gold, purple, green, silver streamers hung above our heads crisscrossing, intertwining, wrapping around each other hanging like canopies. Balloons suspended in the air telling us what we were celebrating (Mardi Gras) and what year it was (20—). Litters of female students gathered in their respective cliques bunched up tightly laughing out loud discussing school, boys and hair. While, not too far, were the packs of male students, each waiting for the right moment to pounce, shooting the shit about football, cars and money. The cougars, fewer in numbers, scattered about the terrain gave advice to each other on how to capture a man and how to keep them, all the while most of them secretly thinking they're Samantha Jones. Among them all were the classic hunters, not like the college guys, but rather more refined in technique and skill knowing they could have a cougar, a gazelle, or a kitten depending on their mood. These hunters would glide through the bar sneak through the brush watching for the perfect kill. And within this superficial joke of a jungle, we found our way to the watering hole to get a drink of the ever-flowing waterfall of suds.

We ordered drinks just as in any establishment that had an Irish ring to it. Tammy the owner took our orders wearing a mask in conjunction with the celebration while the other two male bartenders had none. Tammy would sometimes leave it on the top of her head when counting money but eventually dispensing with it altogether. She was a gazelle on her way to becoming a cougar, wherever those ages lie I don't know but I would never question it. Mike, closer to the bar, would try to hit on her later in the night after we've all had a few. All I wanted to hit was the memory of Shusha and hope alcohol would knock it out of the park.

I was maybe expecting music of some New Orleans Jazz Jamboree nature, being in the spirit, but from the speakers poured out pop that these college kittens wanted to dance to. It was then I knew they were in the wrong bar and should've gone to some club. A group of them hung around the MP3 jukebox dropping dollars like detergent, you never know how much is enough. These girls had the proper jukebox etiquette down. Owning the music that sets the backdrop for the bar is a responsibility that cannot be taken too lightly. When you're feeding money into that machine, you own that machine for the duration of the song(s); not many people care cause someone will eventually play something different changing whatever was on before. But once you start possessing the jukebox, a different scenario must play out.

There are two kinds of people that have jukebox possession privileges. The first is a generalist; this is the guy (or gal) who likes pretty much anything good that knows the dynamics of the bar and plays what everyone will like for various amounts of reasons. Many of us are generalists because all of us who go to bars know the scene well and enjoy the same kinds of music. And most generalists are alright with relieving position for awhile to let someone hear a couple of songs before returning to action.

But it would not be a generalist who would save us that night. Oh no! It would be the "angry drunk man". This character gets free reign over jukebox possession whether you like the music or not. Picture Nicky Katt in *Dazed and Confused* who wants to "drink some beers and kick some ass" and add a little more rough to his edges. Couple of years ago at a bar Jeff and I go over to the jukebox looking for something to play. A couple of girls happened to be standing behind us, pretty but on the older side. So as we're scrolling we come across ABBA and jokingly say we're going to play some ABBA tunes. The ladies go back to their group while Jeff picked out some songs. When we get back to the guys we hear over everyone this solitary voice, "I'm not listening to fucking ABBA. Take some money and play our songs first. Not gonna ruin my fucking night". We thought it was funny until some poor soul went up to that jukebox and played some number that was not in line with the Alice In Chains and hard core kind of style this guy was going for and so "angry drunk man" laid him out.

It was about after the third time we heard "Gimme More" and one Sporty Spice solo song that this angry drunk guy got fed up and dropped forty bucks into that machine and made up a playlist. There is only so many times anybody can hear "Its Britney, bitch" before you go postal. But these girls may have put it so many times on as a joke, but there are ways of joking with a jukebox that are cool, like playing "Shine On You Crazy Diamond" from *Echoes* or "Echoes" itself; each one twenty-odd minutes and kind of dragging but its okay cause its Floyd. So when "angry drunk guy" turned to go back to the bar, he gave them an eye that said, "Do it and see what happens"; at least that's what I like to think. It actually might have been, "Fuck off". Soon those girls eventually left and we were all for the happier.

We were getting pretty trashed. Jeff wondered if he had the balls to go over and play some songs. He didn't. David kept on about getting back in the game; this being the perfect time to pick any of these females to get over Shusha. I just listened to his rationale about how any of these girls would be lucky to go home with me or rather have me go to their dorm room. Mike, unfortunately, fell in drunken love with Tammy and continued to flirt with her.

"Jeff," I said. "Forget it man. You're never gonna get to play anything."

"I know," he says. "Wishful thinking."

"Forget wishful thinking and start helping me to push Dennis here to get laid," David commented.

"If he wants it, he'll go for it."

"Thank you, Jeff."

"Fine, but how long do we have to see you with a face like Droopy the dog?"

"I'm in a mourning period."

"More like having a period."

"David, forget about chicks right now. Let Dennis do what he wants to do."

I was staring at the television holding onto a pint of Stella trying to get lost to the night. Games, games, games were in review getting ready for the NCAA's March Madness of which teams would possibly make it to the Final Four. Then switching to the NBA games that were on that night and following to NHL and MLB. I paid as much attention to ESPN as Tammy was to Mike. I heard all the stats the commentators gave filling up my head with numbers while I added booze. I could also hear Mike explaining to Tammy what a wonderful time it would be if they got together. On the other side, David induced a brunette studying medicine to take a couple of shots with him, any she desired. She asked for a Buttery Nipple shot. Jeff was too busy talking the menu over with one of the male bartenders to get some Buffalo wings cooked up. Over by the taps the remote sat and I reached over switching the channel to the news. No one, I knew, would ever notice with the hearing impaired words popping up on the television while the volume on mute and most guys at this time where more concerned with trying to pick up the drunk tail to take them home for either one-nighters or new relationships. I didn't want to think about it knowing it might remind me of Shusha. So I kept on drinking while the news people kept talking.

The weatherwoman appeared on the screen with the digital background of New York City informing this world that clouds and freezing winds approaching from the Northwest will make this Spring a cold one. There was a chill traveling down my spine every time the bar door opened to let patrons in or out. My back would straighten out with each icy shot while my face shivered and the cackle of the warm would howl once the door opened to shut it and keep it closed. The blonde gave her five-day forecast with the temperature progressively dropping with a slight chance of snow making its way here straight from the Canadian tundra. And as soon as my head was swimming, I told the guys it was time for me to go and that I'd catch up with them some other time. Stepping out, ice slapped me in the face in the form of winds and I hightailed it to the nearest subway to head on to Penn Station where I could pass out on the LIRR, warm and in peace until I reached my stop to go on home.

MARCH

15th

Winds don't have colors but if I were to give wind a color it would most definitely be blue. And the colder it got the tint would become lighter. So when I say that these cyan winds are really blowing today people would have no need of giving me the funny eye. But it was true, cyan winds began blowing this month and it seemed to be in search of my face. Whether I turned left or right, cyan would find the canvas of my face coloring it red.

My friends were waiting for me while I stood at this bus stop waiting to head out to the city. Dampness still held onto my hair, hanging on since the shower. We hadn't made any plans to do anything in particular just hang out and I was having second thoughts about going out. The wind kept schmoozing the moist cerebral follicles making them hard and tight. A sting began in a tightened muscle in my neck. Then there was a silence. I tried popping my ears thinking that they had clogged and then shimmied my finger in my itchy auditory canal, but silence continued over the sound of traffic and winds. Wiping the earwax on my pants, I heard the crackle of a cigarette behind me and stretched out the pained muscle.

"Beware the Ides of March," I heard coming from an old woman. I turned to look at her with her daughter. She looked ragged, almost beaten by the world, but still kept strong. Her daughter looked middle-aged with blonde hair appearing worked by the cracks in her face and rough hands. They had the same green eyes; the kind of green that can search within your soul. "Beware the Ides of March," she said again. I was confused by those words and couldn't understand if this was directed at me or her daughter. I closed my eyes and upon reopening them they were still there but the old woman was pointing at her eyes. "See there, the eyes of starch." This old hag was informing her granddaughter of her diabetes and what it was doing to her eyes, blindness. She was having trouble seeing and needed help getting around.

A throbbing rhythmically began in my head. Not painful yet, but I believe it was pulsating to the beat of Steely Dan's "Only A Fool Would Say That". The icicles forming tugged at my hair pulling together as many strands as it could. But as the throbbing reached the bridge of the song, the pain started and I decided to go back home. I called up Mike and Jeff (David was working) and told them of my headache. They said they'd stop by later. Falling onto my comfortably cool bed warming up under the covers, I switched on the television.

"Beware the Ides of March," came from the soothsayer on the screen warning Caesar of the day. Strange that now I hear it from the television when earlier I imagined it being said by an old woman who pretty much matched this soothsayer grime for grime. Curious, and in pain, I got up and checked the calendar while finding some Advil. I giggled and popped two pills. Jumping back into bed, I wished for sleep to arrive on her sweet gold chariot to give me dreams. Good ones. Let her flutter through my window and land on the cushioning pillow and whisper words sweet and clear to soothe the torment of my mind.

My brother woke me up announcing the arrival of Mike and Jeff. His blonde curls appeared as a halo around his head falsifying his image of an angel waking my dead corpse for eternal life and I wondered if this is what it was like. To die then reborn into everlasting life with finally expecting your judgment by the mighty judge. Mike and Jeff entered my room; a couple of magi come to praise the reborn king. They asked about my health; I told them I was doing better, that it must've been the weather.

"Yeah, a lot of people get sick when the climate switches," Mike said.

"So anyway, what did you guys do?"

"Oh nothing much. Just the usual walking around. Checking out different things."

"We stopped by Barnes & Noble," Jeff added.

"Oh yeah, I can see that considering you're holding a Barnes & Noble bag."

"Oh very good deduction Holmes," my brother said leaving my room.

"Shut up. Go cut your hair or play with your girlfriend."

Jeff opened up the crackling bag and in his hand produced a paperback flinging it on the bed. I felt the smooth cover of the novel and imagined how my first would feel. Would it have the same texture? Would the smell be the same as a new book's printed aroma? My book was still in the works of being written up. I had about sixty pages but I was about a quarter of the way into the plot.

"Turn it over," Mike said. "You'll find it interesting."

I lifted the paperback and it flopped down and turning it over it flopped down again the other way. As I scanned the cover, horror struck me across the face then laughed. Letters spelling out my name scarred my eyes registering in my brain as a distinction that I had already written a book but, I had never even seen this title or passed it through my mind. I flipped it once again to read the summary and the story was foreign to me. Something about an atomic bomb and some guy, I didn't care about that crap. Then I glanced at the author's mini-bio and there it was; my name once again. No picture. Anger spread over me like melted butter on toasted bread.

"Don't you think it's weird that there's another guy out there with your name doing what you want to do?"

"Yeah, Jeff, it's weird," through my mouth of sarcasm and devious eyes.

"Hey listen guys, do you mind going cause my head's not feeling altogether there right now and I just want to take a rest?"

"Yeah, sure Dennis. But are you gonna be up to going out St. Patty's Day?"

"Mike, I wouldn't want to miss it."

After they had left I didn't want to see anyone. Throwing the book against the wall, I deemed myself to feel better, but of course I didn't. I pulled the sheets over me leaving my eyes to stare at this sore that stared back at me, reminding me that I was just a dreamer who dreamt too big; somebody had beaten me to the punch. The book laughed, heartily and loudly in my head in a steady pattern of half notes in 4/4 time. The melancholy colors of the cover mimicked my mood at this present moment and as they say a dark cloud hangs over you, well these shades laid over me becoming part of my covers. I didn't care that my stomach convulsed, letting loose some gas that was wafting, creeping reached my nostrils. My brother walked back in after hearing the book hitting the wall and asked me if I was okay; I told him I was fine, just tired, needed some sleep, to leave me alone for now, or did he want to smell my gas.

"Alright," my brother said. Looking at me the way he docs trying to analyze the thoughts in my head, his prying eyes were a spotlight on me. From my corner eyes, we saw each other and he got the message and left me to my wallow.

17th

Voracious music laid down the background sounds easing the electronic beats that sampled over popping lights of various hues hanging in the air of this night. Green poured from the walls cascading within the bar and the laughing, sing-a-long sea pretended to be Irish for a day. Some of the people drinking Irish whiskey, Irish vodka and others drinking the green colored beer Tammy concocted. Blue Moon became Green Moon; Guinness was served all around and in glasses promoting the Republic of Ireland.

I was at the bar heading out to be comatose. This type of drinking is to forget everything that's going on. Before, when my friends and I got high, was a substitute for stalling thoughts of Shusha. Now was a time to erase all memories by killing brain cells. Shusha left me and I didn't know what else I could do but mourn my loss. Call me a bitch, but hard men must have some sore spots that call upon tears. What bothered me about it was that she went back to her ex. I couldn't figure out if I did something or acted worse that would drive her to return to where she was before we met. So here I was, trying to drive out her memory using booze cause Lacuna doesn't exist, but it would eventually be similar effects anyway.

But there was no sunshine in creating this spotless mind with my brain as full as the moon and thoughts as bright as the stars. Mike was too busy talking to the ladies. David was keeping watch of March Madness scores while Jeff was waiting to light up. I was alone in my pool of alcoholic bliss. I took swig after swig, shot after shot. Everyone around me was enjoying themselves drinking to the point of idiocy. Tonight those cougars and classic hunters don't come out while the wild young things spread all over this, their time to rule the night. It was not a jungle but rather a storm of college guys taking shots and singing songs and college girls dancing all over the place forging the eye of this hurricane that happens every year.

"Hey Dennis, what's the matter," Tammy asked me.

"My girlfriend broke up with me and I'm just not feeling too well."

"Then why are you out?"

Tammy's eyes looked into mine waiting for an answer. What could I tell her? If I tell her that we broke up in January she might call me an idiot and just go off with her own business. I could tell her it was very recent and I may get a pity fuck. But then my head began with the pounding yet again and I tried not to show it to her. Maybe she sees right through my façade or maybe she's interested, maybe concerned.

"My friends," I replied.

"That's no reason. But I'm not your mother so you do what you want, but try not to be a buzz kill."

"What happened with Mike?"

I asked her before she completely left. She turned her head around swinging her long orange curls and I saw her smile like a ray of sunshine that she might actually say something I want to hear. It was fun for awhile, He's not my type, I don't date clients; any of these would be sufficient.

"He was okay, but I'm just not that interested," was all she said with a swagger like it was she who conquered him and not the other way around.

I was thinking about going after her myself but the

pounding of a heartbeat heavy as a jackhammer erupted in my brain. Another drink was placed in front of me but Tammy wouldn't accept my money. I dropped it down quick. Liquid swishing around while rolling across my tongue and cooling my throat. Trying hard to keep the pain at bay which would hide away for a few minutes then return again just as bad as it had left. Then I'd need another drink. Then I'd think of Shusha and order another.

Staring into the faces of these beautiful evils dancing wearing tight jeans, I couldn't find her face. I found hair, chin, nose, cheeks, eyes in many different faces but not one with the complete package. But of course I knew she wouldn't come around here. This was not her scene. In truth this wasn't our scene either, but we weren't going to let uni-students take over our hangout spot. And the view of ladies wasn't bad either. But my libido was not set in torpedo mode so I had no interest in any of them unless they looked like Shusha.

"How you doing?"

Mike came over to check on me. I could smell the mixture of perfumes that lingered about him copulating with his cologne. The strong stench gripped my nose and tried to rip it off while my throat got that vacant feeling when you want to throw up. My eyes watered a bit as it flamed up.

"Oh," I gagged some. "I'm doing alright."

"I got a couple females waiting."

"Wait a minute. What about Tammy?"

"Oh, she won't care."

"Why not," I was curious.

"Look, we hooked up for a bit but it was just for fun.

Nothing serious. She was just another territory on my quest to tap a female from every country." Some men want to conquer the world through force and war, Mike wanted to conquer the world through its women. "When you have a woman from another country, you don't just make love to a woman. You're making love to that country, making love to history, to culture."

"But what about those girls you got over there. Were they born here?"

"Yeah, but the thing is that once they've been Americanized, it's not the same anymore unless they feel nationalistically linked to their roots. Like they kept the culture alive within them. Tammy was just an Irish notch."

"She feels like she got you."

"Then we've helped each other. Come on."

Mike was still pushing me to go over and maybe be a wingman. I was not in the mood, but Tammy warned me not to be a buzz kill. I looked over at these American-born foreign minded females and surrounding them was this American tradition of being Irish and getting trashed. They all emerged from the crowd, appeared as a Whitney Houston 80's video on crack and my stomach convulsed. All the bright colors.

"Hey guys," Jeff showed up. "When can we go to the bathroom and you know."

"We're not high school girls." Jeff rolled his eyes. "Come with me and talk to these girls, Dennis' not feeling alright."

"Alright."

Jeff, I knew, would find some action guaranteed. He'd probably ask these girls to smoke up and make it easier for

Mike. Whether Mike cared about that type of conquest I didn't know. Less energy in playing and more for the fun, I guess. But while they were with the catches, David came by and ordered a shot for each of us. Tammy came by dropping off the shots and gave me a look that she warned me and indicated her indifference. David tilted his head before I even had a finger on mine.

"Fucking UCLA!"

"What's the matter?"

"Tammy. Two more."

"What happened?"

"That fucking gorgeous team had an incredible season and they fucking choke in the semi's!!! I don't fucking believe it!!"

"That sucks."

"How do you have a superior team like that and become amateurs when its important?! Fuck!"

I've never been an avid sports aficionado but anyone can tell when something good goes bad.

"Come on, come on. Drink up."

"How much did you lose?"

"Nothing really, just a couple hundred."

My head began to swell with the shots. Eyeballs tried pushing themselves out of my sockets. I felt tears running down my cheeks or was that the tequila residue left in the glass David slammed on the counter sprinkled on my face. The bridge of my nose tightened and my throat expanded. Light-headed, I got up with muscles swimming within my skin like Jell-O. The bar started getting smaller and people started crowding me. I believe I was drunk but the illness got hold of my immune system and roughed it up. I couldn't see Jeff or Mike through the forest of skin but I let David know that I had to leave and that I was going home. When the green started to shake, I knew I was right for leaving. David asked if he should come along to help me. I replied I'd be alright and thought I was until I walked a few blocks and realized I needed to use a toilet. The question of the day: Do I find a bathroom or do I go at it like a dog?

I walked on for a couple of more blocks checking windows for lights to any place that I hoped would be open. My stomach started to act up rumbling and tumbling with no clear sign of hope. A soft ball with the weight of a bowling ball sat where my bladder used to be. And the night got colder as it darkened. I was no longer walking but hovering as if my legs didn't exist. The sidewalk just flew beneath me while I zoned in search of a latrine. The pounds in my head weighed heavier as well and kept on striking without pause which of course didn't help any either. Then shaking arms, legs (they came back), torso and head appeared. I soon found an alley.

As I grabbed the corner of the brick building, I swung in and everything came flying out. Vomit is not necessarily a projectile since your head is bent facing the porcelain goddess. Being upright walking and the object in motion theory applies, I proved the theory true. Coming to a halt as bodily functions were in motion, I saw this pinkish or greenish, I couldn't tell which, sludge shoot ten feet forward. And because my body and mind were so concentrated on throwing up, my legs gave out and so did my bladder. Now I was wet to add insult to this injury. Muscles did not want to move as well as being too cold to move. From this point on is a blur, I don't remember how I made it home but I did and everyone who came across would've smelled piss and vomit. I guess that's a normal ending to this blessed event.

After the St. Patty's Day massacre on my carcass, I knew I wasn't fit to work. So I called in sick for the rest of the week. The secretary thought it was a one day recovery session and mentioning that Mr. Cotton wouldn't like it very much but I explained to her my situation in disgusting detail and her responses came faster as she tried desperately to get off the phone. But I was in bed, stuck, with no knowledge of if I'll ever use my cadaver again.

Days passed by and my fever ran up and down coasting through my cells. I felt this growing pain circling my stomach like a galaxy just spinning within nothing, with no destination or sign of stopping in sight. The pain made silence audible making creaks louder making ears ring making arms grab stomach making hands grab head making body light. Sweat. Pouring out of me made me cold making me freeze all over again making me try to heat my body sweating again in cycle. Tea and soup was given to me. But as I gulped it down that pain would force me to rush to the toilet as diarrheic friction burned my ass. At times my ass would push and there would be nothing.

Then once again I called in sick the next week saying I was not over my illness. At one point my boss called me. He sounded peeved.

"What the hell's the matter with you?" You could hear his shortness over the phone. His Napoleonic stature was in his voice while my sound stood two feet over his but with being ill I heard his tallness. I imagined seeing him in his suspenders talking on the phone with his 40/40 spectacles and thin hair flying in his face. He'd be sitting behind his desk with his lips hung open while listening to what I had to say.

"Now Mr. Cotton, I've been sick for the past week and a half with whatever it is I've got..."

"You know you left work undone."

"Mr. Cotton, I'm the janitor. What work was left undone if all I do is clean and had to be clean by the end of the day to be ready to be cleaned the next day?"

"Listen, don't get funny. You know full well you have to empty the metal chips and that wasn't finished."

"Well couldn't the night guy do it?"

"Remy *has* been doing it."

"I don't understand the problem." My head began to hurt with the go nowhere conversation.

"You don't have anymore sick days and you've taken too many already."

"But I can't work if I'm sick."

"If you want to keep your job you will."

My head got lighter at that point. And I couldn't help thinking about nothing but wanting to get him off the phone. I couldn't care less about who did what or if it was ship-shape clean. He and the company could all go to hell.

"Listen here, Dennis. I suggest you find a way to heal up quick if you want to continue working here. Understand?" Then he hung up.

'Yeah, yeah, yeah, fuck you' was my response thinking he could hear though the call was over. I dropped the phone to roll over and pass out. The job was getting done whether I was there or not so it didn't matter who did it. But after a couple more days, Mr. Cotton called me again.

"Dennis! What did I tell you?! Do you want to lose your job?"

"No." I sounded wrecked. Tired and hoarse with stomach cramps who could be in the mood to talk about such trivial crap when your health should be more important.

"I suggest you get your act together. And also..."

I tuned out for a bit. I pictured him sitting once again behind his desk but this time getting a hand job from his secretary ten years his junior. His suspenders, pants and underwear lying at his ankles and his Johnson upright with her fist closed around it riving up and down and taking notes with the other. His heavy breath came pumping through over the line.

"Did you get all that Dennis?"

After I came back to reality, I couldn't take it. It was either him or me.

"You know what, Mr. Cotton? You know what?"

"What?"

"Fuck you! Fuck you and fuck your job! And tell Shirley to get off her knees and not to go down again until you get her some kneepads." And I hung up. All I could think about then was the stupid look he would have on his face eyes all bugged out that somebody would say such a thing turning to Shirley just as she's topping him off using his shirt to clean her self. It's funny that now I was expressing what I felt. I'm working at a job I hardly understand that's beginning to get on my nerves. It's horrible trying to do a job when you half know what you're doing and twice as bad when you get yelled at for not doing it. It doesn't take a genius to be a porter but it was never for me. When I was healthy, work didn't bother me, just hold it all inside. But once you take the barrier away, out comes the truth. And so, I laughed and I knew my janitorial career was over.

My brother came in carrying my mail one day. He separated the envelopes and tried to hand it to me but I motioned to him to the pile on the floor next to the bed. He dropped it on the group of about twenty and shook his head. I held that journal in my hands reading over my stories hoping to work on it but knowing in my state nothing would come of it. Part of me thought it was good while another told me it wasn't even worth writing down and should be burned. Regardless, I wanted to burn the book that represented her. And all this journal did was remind me she left.

"You know these are bills you forgot to pay?" my brother said to me.

"Yeah, I know."

The bills overdue from the Shit-mas present had been paid for late but with the New Year slap in the face and the Valentine's deterioration, forgetfulness had come over me but its not all just memory loss. I'd paid what I could and time after time my money disappeared on me dwindling with every bill and that's when "I didn't forget but didn't want to remember" got me. I knew my brother wouldn't steal from me. It was just a stupid thinking. I didn't want to think about them. But there they were, lying at my feet, growing ever so slightly looking up at me expecting to get something as a child would a parent. But they had no innocent look though it was a white envelope, the red highlight reading "Overdue" and "Collection Agency" stared at me burning a hole in my thoughts. I knew I was inside my own economic depression.

"When are you going to do something about them?"

"When I can get out of this bed to do some work."

A pain started up again in its rhythmic beat and my eyes pulsated in unison. The walls felt closer and the covers got hot. Pushing them away, I told my brother to just leave the mail and go. I told him I wasn't feeling too well and the conversation was dragging my strength.

"It's not the conversation," he told me. "It's the room."

Then he walked out. I, left there alone with my thoughts leading from what I've written and what must be done to take care of my life but it slowly running out of control because the reins were not in my hands, sat there with no feelings, in the sense of what to know what to understand of what was going on, staring into space that I knew was my journal. That lightness, which is another type of feeling, came over me once again beginning from my arms, the journal dropped, moving through my torso to my legs. I got cold and pulled the covers over me and I figured I had menopause without the uterus. Then I thought quickly for a minute what if I were to disappear, to completely go away forever, never to know the aches of disease or stress of debt or even the hurt from life. Why Hamlet never went through with it was ridiculous. He still ended the same way. A lot of good it did him to try to prove his father's murder if it meant his life. And he went through the agony of his own mind, when he could have just let it go and live a full life. But here I am thinking of the same solution, for what, to get out of just the act of living life. There are times though when the answer looks just that good. Some may not understand but it's not for groups to understand, just individuals because you know your reasons. All this running through my head with scissors, I fell asleep.

sequence the dream sequence the dream sequence the dream
The court room, crowded with thousands, was noisy loud with words tossed around going to ears of those who tried to pay attention. Fluorescent light hung high blocking out the dark ceiling, squinting you could see the quill painted upon it. The rough columns circled round the room gleaming white in their Doric style. There were no pew-like seats but folding chairs, arm chairs, and all kinds of chairs as per the sign by the front door, B.Y.O.C. (Bring Your Own Chair) while others without them stood alongside the walls. Over the sea of heads sat the judge and next to him the jury box. And there in front of his booth was a lone chair fenced off and raised five feet from the floor; all the furniture dressed up in mahogany. Commencing the trial from the back, I walked into the courtroom reluctantly pushed in by two guards.

"Mr. Bock, do you know why you are here?" yelled the judge over the murmurs.

"No I don't your honor," I yelled back.

"Then come on down," as he waved me over and pointed to the chair. "And we'll play 'What's My Crime?'"

The beefy, trench coated guards forcefully guided me through the crowd. Driving through everyone, I wondered if Josef K felt so solitary when he walked in this sea of words coming from all angles. I couldn't make out what anybody said as they all converged together creating gibberish garbage in my ears. Few words made it through like 'despicable', 'villain', and 'incorrigible'. The guards unlocked the gate and sat me down on the chair.

I recognized the entire jury. They were all dressed

according to their place in history and almost every one of them eyeing me as they couldn't decide to find me guilty or innocent before anything of this show began. Jane Austen, looking beautifully gowned, winked at me; maybe she likes the dangerous type of guy. You wouldn't know with the books she writes. Henry Miller sat there pretty Stoic waiting to hear the case lighting up a cigarette. Cycloptic James Joyce took down notes without even once noticing me. Burroughs was there too chewing on an apple speaking to the courtroom boy standing by the jury box taking orders for lunch knowing that this case was going to take all day. The Great Loretsi, Hovhannes Tumanyan, was next to The Bard discussing literary skill from tragedies that they've written. Escaping from his sickbed for the event and his civil duty, Marcel Proust asked his nurse to hand him some medicine while he would take his tea and offered some to Gabriela Mistral who accepted. Agha Shahid Ali looked round the room as much as I did for his first appearance at one of these things since being dead for a few years. Hemingway, the foreman, informed Ali the way this case was going to work and I couldn't even hear a word. Falling asleep in his seat, the blind Homer snored away as César Vallejo with his stone cold face was pissed to be next to him eyeing the snot hanging from Homer's nostril.

From the courtroom door labeled "Lawyer Entrance" came in Dostoyevsky dressed in a plebian uniform of black and attached to his face was the Orthodox beard to go along with it. He had a slow strident walk, no strutting just tired. The eyes were awake, alert while his body was decaffeinated.

Strolling in after him, Tolstoy in tan told a trench coat truncheon intimately something secretive so this soldier shook hands and strolled out. Tolstoy, too, wore the Russian beard with pride and, unlike his foil, it was trimmed properly. Taking off his beige gloves, he reached out and shook hands with Dostoyevsky. The latter evened out his mouth and bowed his head in respect. Tolstoy flipped a coin that landing on heads they parted.

"Sirs, which of you will go first," asked the judge.

"I shall your honor," Tolstoy replied. Then the entire court hushed down awaiting the commencement. "This man here," pointing at me, "has committed a terrible crime." He went into detail of the words 'terrible' and 'crime' and what they meant. "So yes, I say, a terrible crime. And what crime is that, ladies and gentlemen of the jury?" He paused for dramatic effect until the single word crept from his lips resonating around the court. "Ladies and gentlemen of the jury, your honor, and ladies and gentlemen of the entire court," another pause, "I implore you to please pay attention to the victim who is here to speak for himself." Gasps could be heard all around. "Yes, the victim is here for your ears. And I should hope that the jury, as well as you," talking to the audience, "will find this man guilty of first degree murder. Thank you."

It was then that I knew why I was here. And I knew that this sixteenth century author was to defend me. Dostoyevsky patted the rail of my booth as he stepped forward to embark on the journey of my defense.

"Ladies and Gentlemen of the jury, crime, itself, is a reflection of what comes from the insanity of society. In a case such as this one, for Mr. Bock, who spends all his time pondering on one thing all the time, as a monomaniac would, becomes cold and uncaring until he cares nothing for humanity. But there are also two opposing characters within him fighting for superiority. There's a goodness in him too and for such an act to be committed is just a logical error in his thinking, a mistaken view of ideas. And one more thing ladies and gentlemen to conclude my speech, I tell you that suicide is no crime though my counter would have you think otherwise." And he sat down.

Murmurs and gasps and fainting filled the room. People were saying it all over, "suicide". And I was confused. What could Dostoyevsky be thinking? How could I have committed suicide if I was sitting right here and let alone there was a victim behind door number one waiting to be presented to the public to tell his tale of how I "murdered" him. Which was it, suicide or murder? Albert Camus was sitting there front row to watch how this would all pan out.

"This will be helpful to my findings and research," said Camus taking notes.

"Why do you?" asked a man with rough hands next to him.

"Because clearly this man is not killing himself because he has no reason to live but rather killing himself to have a life. Don't you have a boulder to push?"

"Yes, but its on its way down so I've got time to kill."

"Order," the judge shouted banging the gavel. "Order here! I will have order!"

As soon as the court quieted, the judge announced to Tolstoy to bring out his first and only witness, the other me. My eyes turned to the door, locked to see who it was that would walk out. But I wasn't the only one. A great shift of heads in a single wave turned to the left each one wondering along with me.

The door cracked open and more of the shocked gasps spread over and I turned around yelling "Oh come on" and turning back to that person at the door "This can't be". Standing there portraited within the doorframe was this other me, though it didn't look like me, I knew it was me. He was an imitation of Jonathan Rhys-Meyers but the charge of energy that attracted me and the crowd made all of us believe it was me. Mad, I lunged off my seat and over the railing to tear off what I thought was some sort of mask and an uproar exploded. Tackled by the guards I was claiming liars and conspirators of the whole court to have this imposter pretend to be me. I called out for a mistrial and other such nonsense. The judge battered the gavel with all his force screaming of order and to keep me restrained in my chair. I objected and yelled 'conspiracy' and one of the guards shot me with a fist to my jaw and I shut up dizzy.

After the excitement, all eyes were upon it, the other me. It was sitting in the witness box all calm, collected and classy. Tolstoy walking over offered a cigarette; it accepted. A series of questions followed that it began answering courteously. Its name was my name. Its occupation was my occupation. Everything was falling in line. Family, Friends, and even Shusha. Then the difference sprung from its lips. It had written a book. I had never written a book yet. I turned to Dostoyevsky. He put up his hand as if he knew. Then Tolstoy asked it to describe what happened on the night of the so-called murder.

It began by describing how I tracked him down to take revenge of stealing my lover, literature. It said I walked inside telling it that it was my house and my things and it hadn't even earned it all. It had made me sound like a madman, some David Berkowtiz or Mark David Chapman. What made me irritated was it started to tear up, actually begin to cry. It then talked about the scuffle and finally how I plunged a knife in his chest. Repeatedly, due to the passion of the crime. Silence was lounged in the court but I couldn't allow that to happen. So I began clapping.

"Bravo," I stood up. "Wonderful performance. There's a slight problem with your testimony buddy."

"What's that?" It had nerve to ask.

"You're still alive."

It then proceeded to open its shirt and show the court the wounds left on his person. I still laughed explaining a little Hollywood make-up could work wonders. But when I stopped, everyone became stiff. Statuesque and couldn't (or wouldn't) move. I walked down from my box, touching everyone but not one batted an eyelash. Then out of the crowd, a little girl came skipping along singing.

"Sand castles never stay," she sang without acknowledging my existence. "Tides come to wash away." And she repeated it over and over just moving through the courtroom.

"That's Pippa passing through," came a voice behind me. I turned around; it was sitting in its box and jumped down to the floor.

"I thought Pippa sings something else. And was in Robert Browning's story or something."

"Pippa is in everybody's story but sings something different for everyone."

"Who are you?"

"Now you sound like the caterpillar."

"Whatever, but the question still remains."

"I'm you. You're me. We are one in the same."

"No."

"Yes. Is it that hard to believe considering there's another writer with our name and our father shares our name as well."

"Okay. Then what is this?"

"This is the *volta* in your life. The change, the turnaround. In Italian sonnets it happens in the middle of the poem. For Shakespeare at the end."

"How do you know about the other writer?"

"Uh, I told you. I'm you. And what are we going to do about him?"

"What do you mean?"

It, or I, explained to me that he, the writer, was the cause of my particular situation. No job, No money, No girlfriend, No health, No dreams.

"It's what happens when dreams turn to ash."

"What?"

"Ash. When everything you want and long for, worked for, is suddenly taken away, those dreams that you once had about your future, turns to ash. There's no more hopes, no more dreams."

It, or I, began to make sense. The dream I wanted was hardly lived cause I realized someone else was living it. But even through the understanding, all that I could think of was that this was crazy.

"Madness doesn't just fall upon you, it builds up to the point of the last straw before it blows up," he said.

Me talking to myself, face to face.

"No different than talking in front of a mirror."

There's no way this was possible. I couldn't believe it.

"Look, believe it. I'm here, you're here. And he's there." A map of the world shot down and he pointed to Toronto. "There's only one thing to do. We both know it has to be done. He stole our life before we had a chance to live it."

"He stole our life before we had a chance to live it," I repeated.

We mantra-ed that one line over and over until I began to believe it. My religious prayer, my psalm of psalms.

"Now wake up."

I was in my room coughing, wheezing; my brain pounding three tons of pressure inside. Ran to the toilet to throw up whatever solid was left in my body. The cold tile attempted to comfort me as I laid down.

I knew what I had to do. It spoke to me from the inside. Literally. So, getting up as best I could, making it over to the computer stumbling through pain in the brain, pain in my legs, pain in this stomach I googled my name. Nothing. Searched once again using the middle initial. Nada. My eyes lazily painfully crossed over the desk to the floor where the book lay, then I typed once more, just my given name and surname. And there it was on wikipedia, DENNIS BOCK.

PRINT.

There was no photo available but asked if I had one to please insert. So checking my documents going into my pics, I placed the best one of myself in the box. It was the right thing to do. To continue, I clicked on EDIT and fixed my information. But changing the wikipedia page to suit me was not enough. The physical book was a reminder that he still existed in this far off land; whether it was Mordor, Narnia or Canada, the fact remained that he was alive and lived in Toronto.

Googling once again, I found a site that was all his. A black background with four blue boxes and written, in green, were BIO, PICS, BOOKS, CONTACT. There were quotes from his books, I guess, written around the site. I didn't pay attention to them. I was only interested in information. I read the biography and it repeated much of what was on wikipedia. Clicking on PICS next, there were pictures of a retreat house out in the woods of Toronto. But still not a single photo of him. A nice lake or pond with the caption, Great Fishing Hole, but not one portrait. Then I checked his contact info and wondered if he would be stupid enough to put up his own address for others to find him. He wasn't. All that was there were a simple P. O. Box number, town and zip code which I noted anyway.

Then I stared at the final box to click. Part of me didn't want to do it, figuring it would enrage me further. And for that reason, the other part of me did. But I was scared of what to find. A man who was me to have written so many books before I got my chance would have depressed me. But there were only four books. Three, two novels and a collection of short stories, already published. The fourth, 'in progress' the caption blinked. I thought he was no more a writer than I. All he has was age. There was no more timidity within me. He was my equal, a contemporary in which I show contempt.

Checking underneath the mattress, I retrieved whatever

money I had saved. I decided all I need were some clothes since I was only going to discuss the proposition to end his writing farce and look into another profession. And maybe a little intimidation. So I prepared myself for the journey Friday and waited for the next day to pack.

3

"APRIL...

...is the cruellest month."

—T. S. Eliot

My brain felt like a giant weight sitting in a 100-degree oven as my own mass sat in the train perspiring a little. Inside of this tin can, I was staring out at Planet Earth floating off to wherever and I knew how Major Tom felt. I had to admit the seat was pretty comfortable considering the cushion must have been fifty years old as the fabric was gradually peeling off with age. The window felt cold enough to place my head upon it to cool myself down but the train's movement hurt so no comfort lay there. I hoped they'd turn on the air conditioner like I asked but I think the ticket handler just looked at me funny. Said something about the weather being chilly to turn it on. In other words, she was telling me that I was a little wacky.

Not a lot of noise, besides the racketing of the tracks, most passengers remained silent. Conversations that did fill the air were loaded with familial discussions of what to do when they reached their destinations, who had to go potty but didn't want to touch the seat, and who was hungry now and didn't want to wait for later. Other debates between adults were about the spiraling down economy and how Obama's bill didn't stimulate any wallets while the advocates claimed it was due to the people's lack of willingness to spend money. While traveling along the Hudson, someone said that Obama should get Captain Sully at the helm of the damaged economy.

After the various stops along the river and catching a glimpse of West Point, we made a refuel stop in Albany and, as it was customary for passengers to vacate the train, I had to get off though my body said it couldn't. When you're on your way to pull a crazy stunt like gliding off the Empire State Building or even suicide bomb a plane, you don't want to get noticed before the big moment. Its like premature ejaculation with a virgin, you reveal the secret before it's due. And, as sick as I was, I didn't need anyone noticing me.

The moment my foot hit the pavement my body went into weak mode. My organs were melting their way to my feet and my balloon brain held me up hovering over the floor. I willed myself into the station house to the lavatories and finally into a stall where acidic liquid flew from my facial orifice. Once my stomach was relieved I situated my mass on the toilet to regenerate the lost energy and sure enough I closed my eyes.

Upon reawakening, the sound of the whistle echoed through and the concrete in my shoes refused to budge. My torso limped forward and bobbed my head until I was lying on the tiled floor. I slowly moved the stall door back and urged myself to go forward. Inch by inch whatever remained of me was like The Blob on the move. I even felt gelatinous. But I pushed on, hearing whistle upon whistle after another and making it to the door I pulled. My hand, the knob and any bicep strength I had left raised me up. Nausea returned to tempt me back into the stall. But it would have to wait. With atrophied bones cracking, I made it out the door.

Standing by the vending machine, every part of me froze. My eyes could see passengers boarding and the announcement for "All passengers to Niagara Falls are boarding now" filled my ears. People brushed up against me saying "excuse me". My muscles were afraid to move. And from the back of my mind suddenly I heard myself telling me, *"Let's go. We've got work to do."* A leg took a step. Then the other. And so on until a walking motion began that seemed more like a drunken strut.

"All aboard," yelled the conductor. And as he helped me on, "Hey, we almost left you behind."

"You left him in the city." And I stumbled to my seat.

The train pulled out of the station and we were on our way. In the distance, the mountains were real, stationary, and scenic. They knew what they were and accepted it. Nothing else for them to do, just be. While up close, the view passed by like a reel. Each frame seemed imagination made real by set production, and the playback in my head saw farms and homes and edifices as pieces on a model train platform. Watched the clouds disperse to see a naked sky revealing the emptiness that surrounds this world knowing there is nothing more. My head moved to a different thought; a thought that had burrowed and found a home in my cerebellum slightly gophering before but now stuck its head out to guide me. I pulled out the address, though a P.O. Box, it told me the town and zip I had to search out. The reason for my trip North. To hunt for the imposter.

The day grew longer as the sun struck noon and I knew night was soon to follow. But by three we made it to Niagara Falls, New York. The station and the area looked bitter, a middle-aged man with nothing to show for his years gone by, just keeps on trudging along through life. That was this station. A highway overpass just next door didn't care for its purpose; it knew it was doing its job. The conductor announced that there will be a short pause to wait for the train in front of us to cross the bridge. My head was still swimming in nausea, the clouds, and the hunger that I couldn't satisfy, the thirst I couldn't quench, the movement I couldn't project. I wanted so much but my body refused. *Not until the deed is done.*

"What are you talking about? We're just going to tell him to stop writing," I said to myself. *But do you think he'll stop?* "He better," I said worried he wouldn't. *Yeah for his sake he better.* "No, he better cause its not right. Two writers with the same name cannot exist." *That's stupid. Many people have the same name.* "So?" *You know what has to be done.* "No I don't." *We'll see.*

Footsteps could be heard shuffling to find seats while bodies left cars meeting friends, loved ones at the station. I knew I wouldn't be received that way once I arrived in Toronto. Obviously. There would be no Shusha to kiss me. No Remy to tell me dirty jokes. No brother to hug me. Just as we enter this world, a room full of strangers not knowing anyone, so was I to enter an unknown city to learn what I was suppose to do.

Passing through the invisible wall, we stopped at the opposite station of Niagara Falls. It was a slight mirror image; just a change of appearance that expressed a young man's life with no future posing as a train station. And there, a few uniformed officers in their rigid coats entered each compartment. They found me out. Someone spilled the beans. They were searching for something and I wasn't going to give them any answers. Willingly.

I looked about and saw a couple of them sentry by each exit. No escape. While another couple were walking the aisle stopping at each row asking for information. None of the passengers knew me or my purpose. They should've gotten to me first and forget the delay; we all had things to do. My head swelled and the sitting position upset my legs. The compartment was still too warm. I tried not to look sick but my reflection in the mirror kept giving me away. Then they reached me.

"Your passport please?" The sound was of that French snobbery with British politeness. And one of them took it easily, no rough stuff. But he took his time looking it over. "Where are you going, Mr. Bock?"

"Toronto." I sounded just like I looked.

"What are your plans there?" He was swimming for info.

"Hockey Hall of Fame, CN Tower." I did my research.

"Mr. Bock, you don't look too good," the other one said as he looked me over. "Why go there now?"

"Well, I made my vacation for this time and it was either use it or lose it in my company if you understand." I knew this one's game. I wasn't going to crack under pressure. I thought about this story earlier and made sure my face would be as believable as my words. "As well as the hotel being booked."

"Yes, Mr. Bock, we understand." Then the first one

handed me back my passport. "Do get better. Have a nice vacation." And they both walked on by.

My nerves evened out once they left the train. No captives were taken by the Canadian Gestapo, but there they stood eyeing us as we pulled out from the station to make our final destination. Throbbing tortured my calves for sitting too long, while my brain continued its never ending Bataan Death March of Pain. I got up to walk around but my legs were going to give out on my way to the separation between cars and I made it to the toilet in time to fall to the floor.

There I sat facing the bowl my legs outstretched on either side. My head searched for the right position to relieve the expanding tension. The shocks of the train vibrated beneath me but at the time I thought back spasms finding their way through my legs. Then finally, with epileptic fervor, my stomach relieved itself of the bile left over. The rapping at the door rang in my ears and I could only respond that I was busy.

Knowing I had to leave the lav or else there would be talk, the muscles of my remains forced themselves to move, to rise, to exit and return to the decay of the seats. Around me, the world started slipping away while beginning this imploding process that would never reach its conclusion. My flesh sucked into itself but stayed stagnant. An itch appeared and my arms were too busy being folded that they couldn't wrap around to scratch. And the itch spread from point A, my left shoulder, on to point B, my right, stretching to points C and D of my lower back. The itch switched to a shiver sticking to my torso. There was nothing I could do so my exasperated energy only finally shut me down to make an attempt at recharging.

When I awoke, we had arrived at the Toronto station and the moon had traded places with the sun. Looking around, some passengers were already getting their bags together while others vacated. From my seat, I saw the meets and greets of families, businessmen and friends. And as the cliché goes, I felt lonely in a crowded place. Every part of me continued to ache but I got up anyway and collected my bag. There was nothing but clothes. I didn't even know what clothes; I just threw shit in.

The station was bright with fluorescents illuminating all across the floor from wall to wall leaving hardly a shade in sight. The flashy signs of stores calling out to customers enticed them to enter with their colors of green, blue, yellow, red in neon including flashing lights around the word ENTER helped too. And it was clean. You couldn't see garbage cans anywhere therefore no garbage on the ground. The gleam from the tiles showed they'd been waxed and rose to the walls that looked presently washed. And back to the lights, the cleanliness of the station revealed its essence as a bubblegum pop song overexposed on radio, polluted pizzazz with no substance.

The rain pounding upon the windows in rhythm of a dirge equated with my soul. And in the silence between the drops, I tried to hear the truth of why I was here. The reason bounced around in my mind. Maybe a regret. The reason unfolded like a map, a plan that must be completed. Maybe a mission. Whatever it was, it was my journey and I walked out gently into that good night.

Through the streets of Toronto, I knew the destination

but had no clue as how to get there. Aimlessly, I continued moving if only to try to stay warm considering earlier I didn't. So, I laughed. In needing some sort of sanctuary, I stepped into a pub. The atmosphere was like any other. It felt right, like home. I guess it doesn't matter where you go, a pub is a pub. It was dark, kinda dingy. Though some are a tad lighter and cleaner, the furbishing is all pretty much similar between them. Just a bit of feng shui set each one of them apart from the other.

"Wow, you look terrible there," said the bartender. He eyed me up and down. I asked for a pint. "I'm thinking you need some tea." I said no, just the pint. "But you really should drink something warm." So I told him to give me a warm pint and a shot of vodka. "Alright."

I took the shot and walked away. I moved over to the corner to stay out of sight. I took a swig and sat down. I noticed the Irishman sitting close by was in attempt at picking up the young lady next to him. She seemed slightly interested but maybe she was playing the game. He wasn't bad looking but he was a bit sloshed already. I pulled out the address I had for this guy and wanted to, but didn't have the nerve to, ask anyone how to get there. And I couldn't concentrate, being wet and all and the aches still bothering me but what topped it was the brogue and girly laugh in my right ear.

"Listen here darlin', I've got this tattoo of a shamrock," he said. "Would ya like to see it?"

She made this tick tock of her head with raised shoulders to show nonchalantly that yeah she wanted to see it. She asked if it hurt and the other nonsense when discussing tattoos. He said he had to be drunk to do this one in particular while he untucked his shirt. Then while she was questioning where he got it, he showed it to her.

"It's my lucky charm, darlin'," he explained as he held his dick in hand revealing a shamrock on his shaft. "And it's magically delicious."

The shock in a face is priceless when it morphs from a sweet innocent to an ugly mess in under 2.2 seconds. Her eyes in disgust were slapped with terror. The once pursed lips of cuteness now expressed regret for ever talking to such a human being as they shaped themselves like the Coney Island Cyclone. No red cheeks of embarrassment but rather ghostly pale of disgust. After the initial shock, she closed her eyes and repeatedly told him to put away his Johnson. I think I overheard her singing "It's a Small World" but whether she was referring to his size or trying to escape from the moment I couldn't tell. I was in awe of the spectacle and laughed on the inside. But when she came back from Disneyland her tone was not pleasant at all.

"Fucking asshole," as she got up. "I don't need this shit." She gathered up her things but he interjected.

"Darlin', darlin'. I'd a thought you'd wanted to see the goods before we proceeded any further."

"Don't fucking say shit to me. You're just a trashy dick."

"My mouth may be trashy, but I assure you my dick is clean as a whistle. Would you like to blow and find out?"

And he cracked up at his own pun. I began laughing too and when she realized there was an audience present she had to get away. So she did what every female in America, or in the world for that matter, would've done. She gave him a right cross. He wasn't expecting it and he went down.

In my head I yelled timber. And she stormed out the pub. Everyone looked his way as he started to get up.

I wondered about the cycle of men and women. Man acts like an asshole to a good girl. She, in turn, becomes a bitch. She finds a nice guy and treats him like shit. He becomes an asshole and thus the cycle continues. But it's the same story as the chicken and the egg. Who started it first? You could go the church route and blame Eve. Or go the feminist way and blame men for everything. I like *The Matrix* idea better. There's a ninety-nine percent chance of the entire system working. Every so often you get an anomaly that counters the system. In this case, the asshole/bitch are born and do as they please which then webs out to hit many people snowballing to get everyone causing more to be the same, somewhat. Some do realize that it's the wrong thing to do and walk away from that path and others don't. C'est la vie. But also it wasn't just one that began the trouble. Out of millions of people anomalies must've popped up everywhere but we all have that free will to choose which way we want to go.

Stop wasting time; we have a pressing matter. "You're right," I said to myself.

That Irishman suddenly jumped into the seat next to mine and put an arm around me like a friend from the old country. The alcohol emitting from his laughing orifice stung my nostrils and made me sneeze. He toasted my glass and chugged his pint. But that arm of his rested on my wet clothes and increased my irritation as drops ran down my back creating cold lines drawn on my back.

"Hey buddy. How's your night goin'?" I didn't respond. "Let me ask you, do you think it right that she should hit me?"

"You probably deserved it," and I arched my shoulders to get rid of the extra weight.

"Maybe I did," as he took his arm back. Then he saw the directions that I was looking at. "What's this, you trying to get somewhere? I can help you." He grabbed the piece of paper and eyed it squinting as best he could. "I know this area like a dog knows where to shit." Then aimed it in the light to read it a little better. "This looks like Casa Loma. My friend, that's a long way to go."

"About how far," and I coughed. "How long would it take me?"

"You'd need to drive for a bit. But you don't have a car, do you? You could pay a taxi, but," as he took another swig of ale. "It'll cost a bit as well."

He was avoiding the answer for what reason I didn't know. Maybe he wanted to go with me and get a finder's fee for helping me out. Or possibly lure the tourist to a dark alley and rob him.

"Besides, it's a shower outside, you'll get wet."

"If you haven't noticed," I said. I offered my shirt for him to touch.

"Oh thanks, buddy." And he proceeded to wipe his hands. "Towellette is much appreciated."

I couldn't stand it anymore so I finished off my pint and walked out of the bar. The cold rain felt like a great relief from the stuffiness of the pub and the Irishman. My neck ached and in the stretching cracking was heard. I didn't even get five blocks before I heard footsteps coming up fast behind me. After preparing myself, I turned around. It was the Irishman carrying my bag. I left to not deal with him anymore and here he was being friendly. At that point I too wanted to punch him in the face.

"Hey buddy. You forgot this back at the pub."

"Honestly, most people would've taken the bag and called it a day."

"Nah, not here. Toronto's filled with good people. There's shite in there anyway nobody would want." He paused and waited for the response in my face. "I'm joking, just joking. Besides, you're goin' the wrong way. Casa Loma is that way."

We walked on for ten minutes before I understood Casa Loma was not on the agenda for tonight. Arriving at his apartment, he took my coat and bag and set it next to the radiator. He told me to take off my clothes while handing me a bathrobe. Thinking about this situation for several seconds, I wanted out of these clothes but I also didn't want to be violated. I heard him in the kitchen fussing about. The clinking and clanging of metal objects reverbed through the apartment in an unsyncopated rhythm. Sounds bounced off the putrid walls and mediocre table getting eaten up by the rugs and barely making it to my ears.

There was a decent television, Vizio I think, not too big that sat across from the couch where the Irishman and I sat. He handed me a cup of tea to warm me up. But as I drank I thought it tasted funny. There was whiskey involved in this concoction. When he saw my face he said the alcohol will help with the virus. So I drank away.

"Why help me?" I decided to open up conversation.

"Cause its good to help someone in need. I know what its like being stranded almost left for dead without help."

He opened up his shirt and showed me a giant scar that

stretched across his abdomen. He said it was payment from the IRA. When he was around my age in the eighties, he was ordered to plant a bomb and his brother had gone along. He was radical, unthinking about what consequences might come. He knew he wanted a unified Ireland and thought this the only means. So on one morning he placed the bomb underneath a car and set the trigger. I could see his eyes began to tear up and I didn't want him to stop. He remarked that he'd done everything he was told to do but that the bomb maker was a bit of an amateur and put too much explosive and not enough time. When the explosion occurred, the owner was questioning his brother and he had not gotten too far before he turned back to grab his brother. Both the owner and his brother died instantly. The car was torn to pieces flying in different directions and one flew and cut open his abdomen. Bleeding to death, he struggled to get anywhere. It might have been ten minutes or an hour, but he felt an eternity of pain and he passed out. And he poured himself another whiskey and took a shot.

"Eventually someone did call for an ambulance and I woke up in a hospital."

After taking another shot, he began again that the IRA had left him for dead as a martyr. But when he went back, they cheered for only a moment and asked him to continue his duties. When he asked for his brother, they only said he was a casualty and that these things happen sometimes. They told him that his brother shouldn't have been there considering the responsibility. He turned around and said they were recruiting younger boys. They told him that they were being trained before they send them out. It was his own fault that his brother lost his life. They were not responsible.

"What they don't understand is that they themselves are the cause for the effect they want. They are the gun taking aim but we are used as the bullets, cast aside once we're of no use." He paused to pour another. "And I realized that goes with any terrorist group or righteous army, all the leaders who 'believe' are not there doing it themselves."

"And how old was your brother?" I didn't want to ask but it seemed right.

"He was eighteen," as he took another shot. That was the end of the conversation and he had gotten me a sheet and walked out.

Next day I woke up alone in the apartment. I must've slept a long time cause out the window seemed about midday. I walked over to the kitchen to see coffee already made; poured myself a cup. It was a bit cold since it'd been sitting for a long time. I nuked it then strolled around. Hanging on the walls were photos of yesteryear, those of his childhood playing by a creek and on swings as well as growing up when he graduated school and family dinners. Yet every frame contained that ghost of the past that lingered with him. Every face of that young man faded into each picture becoming part of the background. Its easy to forget by erasing people from your life unless you have the scars to remember. It was clear he was trying to forget.

Down the way, a curio stood alone exposing other memories of a torpor past revealing the alcohol-driven present. Mini posters of Parnell sat next to a medal of workmanship that read "Attendance" from some dock in Liverpool along with some recollections of him and coworkers relaxing at the job. Sepia portraits of parents, now gone I guess, were well dressed in their frames. There were photos here of a later life after his brother. A woman with dark hair and light eyes was repeatedly used in every shot. Then one of this Irishman and a baby and that's where the home slideshow section ended.

Towards the bottom lying there in its own glory was a gun. I've seen enough action movies to know it wasn't a revolver, so no Magnum or Colt, or a Lugar cause they look funny. It wasn't a James Bond PP7 either but rather some regular .45 and the black gleam reflected off it when the light hit it right. So I bent down to get a closer look and underneath this weighty specimen was an article. This article specified that a mother and child had been taken out by a bomb planted by the IRA. It was another tragedy that damaged his life due to his past behavior.

My fingers brushed up against the pistol as I tried to read the news of old. The cliché of cold steel ran through my hands like a faucet's run across unclean hands. The electricity of power shot up my muscles inciting brainwaves to imagine such tyranny holding this iron fist. The serfs that would kneel before me willing to serve. But wielding of such a tome requires a mighty hand like Attila or Khan to control it lest the unleashing whirls into a tailspin of trouble. And where it could go is anybody's guess. But still I wished to be its owner. To relinquish its captivity behind glass and let it breathe once more.

Then a jingling of keys and locks brought me back and I closed the curio. I took two giant steps up towards to the door to seem like I was going to the bathroom. My nerves were startlingly shaken. Coming through the entrance the Irishman turned and saw me. He made light conversation on how did I sleep and how I was feeling. I answered the best way I could informing that his hospitality was very kind and generous. I still wasn't well but I didn't let him know that. He'd probably want to keep me here until I was better. *But we have other things planned.* I excused myself to the bathroom. I turned on the faucet and splashed my face. Looking up my reflection looked pissed off.

What the hell are we doing here? "What do you mean?" *We should be looking for that poser of a writer.* "We don't even know where to start looking anyway. And we're both hungry and tired." *I'm not hungry.* "Well, I am. This sickness is taking a toll." *Oh sure, blame the virus.* "Look we'll stake it out until it gets too hairy. He could probably take us where we need to go." *I still think we're wasting our time. But if things don't happen soon I'm coming out.* "What do you mean by that?" Then he was gone.

After drying my face, I couldn't understand what he was talking about. I think I understood. Something Jekyll and Hyde-like except my evil inside looks exactly the same. There'd be no way to fool the cops if something should happen. But nothing will happen anyway. No need to think that way. So I shook my head and met the Irishman in the living room.

"You know this address is only going to take you to a post office?" he said holding the piece of paper in his hand.

"Yeah I know."

Fuck. I had to think quickly about this. What story would I give him? I wasn't prepared for this at all. I didn't know what to do until it hit me.

"It's the P.O. Box for Dennis Bock. He's a writer. I'm a big fan." *Good save.*

"Oh, and you're hoping to meet and what, express your love?"

"God no!"

"It sounds strange to me fella. You coming up here to meet a writer. Sounds a bit obsessed."

"No, not at all." I tried being cool but my nerves weren't helping. "I came up for vacation and I hoped I could run into him. I'm a writer too and I was hoping he would peruse my stuff and give me some pointers."

The Irishman must've bought it cause the interrogation stopped there and we discussed how he would take me to Casa Loma if he didn't have to work but he could give me directions on how to get there. Maybe he didn't buy it and wanted to get rid of me. Who wants a crazy person in their house? Exactly. Then he mentioned it was getting to be dinnertime almost and asked if we should go to the pub for food, drinks and conversation. I said sure and after washing my cup I showered and changed my clothes.

Once there, we ordered whatever ghastly bar food was available to make. Some low version of Buffalo wings appeared as appetizers followed by burgers cooked enough to not be federally restricted by the Canadian government while throughout beer, beer and more beer. Hungry as I was I stuffed it down considering I really didn't have a choice since he offered to pay. I couldn't refuse such generosity; it'd be a slap in the face. And I didn't have that much to begin with anyway.

"So you're a writer?"

"Uhmm…yeah."

"What've you been writing?"

I believe the interrogations had opened up once more.

I kept it light cause I knew divulging too much would hurt me later. No I wasn't published. Yes I've been writing for a long time. I work as a janitor to pay bills. I'm working on a book right now. A murder mystery where two people meet and they don't know that the other is the enemy but also they are the same man.

"But how can they be the same man?" He was good and drunk now.

"Haven't you heard of the idea of the doppelganger?" I believe I was drunk too.

He shook his head.

"The doppelganger is the evil twin. Your complete opposite. One is good, the other evil."

"But won't they know that they are the other?"

"That's the best part, the twist. You see, just because they are your evil *twin* doesn't mean that they have to *look* like you."

His face had the appearance of being shocked at such an idea. The theory of two men being the same rolled around in his brain. Or he had tuned out for awhile from the drinks. Either way, I thought it was a good story and I covered my ass pretty well until...

"So forgive me. I don't even know your name?"

At that moment I was ready to piss on myself cause it hadn't occurred to me as well. I knew what the next logical step was and I debated on whether I should reveal my name. He might not even remember but there was still a chance he could and I'd be screwed. Because of my debauched state of mind, the names in my head were coming at me all at once and not one would stick. But as soon as he asked I was ready.

"Teddy...Teddy Raskol."

The Irishman shook my hand and told me his. I don't recall it anymore but I can only imagine it being traditional like Seamus or Patrick. On we went through the night, whiling away our time in booze and song. Every new track was a new moment to experience and so our lungs exhaled words close enough to the lyrics as the dim lights of the bar replaced the pyre that accepted our prayers and the sacrificed spilt beer to Bacchus. Then soon enough it was time to go. And so we walked on in the rain back to his apartment. The day had changed to...

Palm Sunday - In the apartment, the Irishman left me alone to change his clothes. I followed suit only to get comfortable for bed. My head still swam in the inebriated sea and the Irishman came back with a pen and paper asking if I could write my name down so when I get published he could pick it up. My muscles weakened for I'd forgotten what name he heard. I told him sure no problem and if he could make some tea. As he went into the kitchen, I strangled the cells in my brain to remember. Suddenly it came to me and so I wrote it down.

Simon Raskol.

Then he cam back with the tea apologizing for only having Earl Grey. Assuring him it was fine, I handed him the name and he looked at it strangely. I could read his eyes telling me that he was working something out. My Spidey sense was informing me it was the name I'd written. But he got up and started to the hall when I asked what was wrong. My heart rate began to double up, slowly at first then it went into car speed.

"I thought your name was John?"

"It is. Simon is just my middle name. John Simon Raskol."

"Oh…you're a rascal alright." He threw my name to the floor. "Do you think I'm stupid?"

"No, not at all."

"Then why the sudden name change…*Teddy*?!"

And my heart rate sped up to train mode. He continued walking to the hall telling me that just cause he's drunk didn't mean he had a bad memory. He doesn't have blackouts, he said. That he was being a nice guy and didn't deserve to be lied to. Then I heard a door opening and I remembered the gun. I rushed to the hall and tackled him.

Hands grabbed at faces and throats. Fists connected with chins and chests. It wasn't the most sophisticated bout between opponents but it wasn't the worst either. This was about survival. The Irishman knew it too. He lived through this type of struggle. Though I've had no experience in enduring hardship, primordial instincts take over exciting your body to a period missing in our world. Survival. A long ago blocked memory that only the muscles, bones, nerves only know of but have faded into oblivion surprise you as they appear. The only time it shows its head are in the moments of deep passion and the need to live. Survival. Instances when the animal feels cornered and has the necessity to fight filled me with energy to stop the Irishman in his attempt to prevent my mission. With my knees on his arms, I cupped his head jammed against the wall until the dent in the sheetrock told me he was out cold.

There, lying on the floor was the gleaming piece of metal that had fallen from his hand and I wanted it. My fingers brushed over gripping it tightly and I felt the cool unused aura surrounding it. Felt good, felt right. Before I got up, I checked the Irishman's pulse. He would still live another day so I hid the gun in my pants and locked the door behind me.

I walked on for hours in the beginning of the dark new day. Wet steps squished along the pavement aimlessly moving to nowhere, anywhere. Rain continued to fall upon me in an attempt to cleanse what had occurred. But deep inside me, it didn't matter. The rain was a nuisance and had to stop or go away. Cars drove by without even caring about some stranger walking around at two in the morning in their fine city. It's understandable in New York but Toronto; you'd think they'd worry. Especially if it's raining. Or maybe the city changes at night? Could happen to any city.

My body rekindled its pain. The chill in the bones traveled throughout my flesh creating aches, shaking me in an attempt to heat up. The weight still laid in my head and beat along to its own rhythm. Stopping to cough and sneeze, I heard something.

"Hey!"

It was someone screaming at me. At first I thought of the Irishman had found me out and ready to exact revenge. Within my shivers, I turned my head to see if it was true or a person who possibly knew me. There was this Nissan Altima stopped across the street from me. The face was a blur but I knew he was a stranger.

"You look like a tree standing in water. Do you need a lift somewhere?" he asked me.

"I don't even know where I'm going."

"Well, come on, I'll take you to my house. Get you out of this rain."

I got into the car grateful. The leather seats made the same old sound of screech when wet surface slides onto that plane. There was a fragrance tree hanging from the rearview mirror emitting the scent of Night Music. I could have done without it but it was his car. He shook my hand and began driving. He lowered the music he had playing and asked where I came from. I told him from New York. His face wrote out that he was in awe of how I could be so far away. Not that he could believe New Yorkers going to Canada, but me without a hotel room of some sort. He looked at me, eyeing me to guess something that I couldn't put my finger on. The steel in my waist was colder with the rain but I figured I wouldn't have to use it for this gentleman. Not necessary to bring it out early. I coughed a bit and he said he could read in my face that I needed sleep. In the end, I closed my eyes as his words came to me inducing the incantation to be fulfilled.

When I woke, we were parked in a driveway and this stranger told me we were home. The house was two stories in a slight Tudor sense made with brick. The door creaked from its oak pivoting like a salutation when one enters. The rooms were plain, hardly any paintings to encourage décor, ordinary chairs and tables I assume of oak also, with a bland green grey for a background on the walls. It was a Nick Drake song exposed inside a home, simple with its own quirky twist but still simple. And also kind of uninteresting.

"Please," he pointed out to have a seat. "The chesterfield will be comfortable for you to sleep on. It might be big enough for a person."

The sofa looked pretty modern. One texture to stand out from the tapestry to shake things up. Didn't change the fact it still lacked passion. But it was his imprint on the home. He was fairly rigid and disciplined. He needed excitement and this may have been a release, an escape from the ordinary. But if he tried anything funny I had that piece on deck ready to bat.

In from the kitchen, he asked what type of tea I preferred. I didn't care and so he went back and returned with a kettle, two empty cups, sugar bowl and a couple of spoons on a tray. He poured the tea for both and allowed me my own sugar intake. In the silence, the awkwardness resounded in my head and forced me to open my mouth to begin some sort of conversation but he stopped me.

"I enjoy a good cup of tea before bed. And you look like you need to sleep. We'll talk later on."

And just like that my eyes heavy began to droop. He brought out blankets and pillows as well as some tissues and said his goodnight. After I heard the door lock, I giggled a little and hid the gun underneath the sofa. He had left a robe in the mix of blankets and, after my clothes were off, I put it on. I fixed the couch as best I could and went to bed.

When I next woke it was like nothing had changed. It was still dark and my head began to pound loudly. When this stranger came in, his clothes were different. He told me that it was still Sunday, just at night. He offered a couple Aspirin cause he knew what it was like to sleep for a long period of time. And the fact I was sick didn't help matters. I popped the pills in hopes of relief. Then the stranger offered me a shower and dinner. I was too in need of them that I couldn't refuse or think he'd try something.

His bathroom too was incapable of surprise. All colognes

were neat and in order as were the shampoo and conditioner. The hot water expunged all sensations of the cold rain that I'd been living in for the past couple of days. I could have easily ejaculated just from the water alone but I knew it would require effort from myself so I withheld. I was hoping for the water to do all the work. But, of course, it takes two.

Downstairs, the stranger informed me of putting my clothes in the dryer and I could eat in the robe. Wasn't a big deal. I got worried. But I went along. During dinner, he asked me my name and I told him Simon Raskol and on this occasion it was going to stick. Then he asked about the food, if it was good and if I'd like some wine or would tea be better. I said the Chicken Milanese was fine and that either wine or tea would do. He kept the conversation focused on the moment without gearing to anything of depth. Through his words, I looked into his face seeing he was in his forties and the short hair and clean shave made the attempt to appear younger. I only had the one glass to keep my head in the game this time. And once we were done he said we'll have tea in the living room.

"Now, my dear Simon," he said as he finished pouring the tea. "As Alcinous asked of Odysseus, tell me your tale."

I had to spin another ball of yarn to keep him at bay from interrogation. I couldn't have what happened with the Irishman occur twice. It wouldn't help with my plans, leaving a trail of injury for that Gestapo to follow. The bruises were from me getting robbed and trying to defend myself. But I let him know that I was lost looking for a fellow writer, traveling up to Canada for research and hoping for relaxation. And once I mentioned about being a writer he jumped on it.

"Ah, so am I," he excitedly put down his glass. "When April with his showers sweet fruit, The drought of March has pierced unto the root, And bathed each vein with liquor that has power, To generate therein and sire the flower." When he saw I was unsure of what he was saying or doing he explained. "Geoffrey Chaucer."

"Nice," as I thought it was a bit old. After using some tissues I tried to reciprocate in my own way. "April is the cruellest month, breeding Lilacs out of the dead land, mixing Memory and desire, stirring Dull roots with spring rain."

"Eliot...very nice. Some Modernism is fine, but the older bards knew how to string words together. But anyway, I'm more of prose anyway. I thought I'd impress you with some poetics."

Then he asked what type of book I was writing and if I've ever been published. I told him that I hadn't even met a publisher before and the book was kind of personal. He offered his services to edit it if I was any good and gave a snicker. Then he asked about the writer I was visiting. I returned with not knowing who he was but only a name.

"What is it?"

"Dennis Bock."

His eyes lit up glowing along with the candles from the dining room. He wanted to know why I was searching for him. I informed him that I was interested in discussing some things with him about literature. And because of his reaction I figured he knew him. So I asked.

"Of course I know him...I'm he!"

Shock shot shivers through me when this imposter revealed himself. He began talking about some garbage I wasn't even interested in. My mind was involved in his books and wikipedia site and the fact that he was living *my* dream.

I calmed myself down and tried not to go overboard. I explained to him who I really was. He didn't understand and tried to make it out. I knew then it would not go over well. *You're an idiot.* Insulted that I lied to him he got up and wanted me to leave. Trying to be civil, I wanted to impart my theory of him writing and the impediment it causes mine. He refused to pay attention to anything I had to say. He demanded that I leave. And I said not until I've said what I had to say.

"Well say it and get out!"

"I want you to stop writing! You writing and me writing doesn't work! You're living my dream!"

"That's insane and now get out."

"Are you going to stop?"

"Of course not. That's preposterous. Now get out before I call the police."

I sneered. Deep within me my other self came out like a lion pouncing on him, I attacked without convention. My fist connected with his jaw. And he hit me in an attempt to do damage to my person. He struggled to push me off and ran for the cups and threw whatever he could. I jumped over him and dropped down to grab the gun and slapped him with it. He stopped dead as I took aim. Fear was written in his face. We got up slowly.

"Turn around."

"What are you gonna do? Kill me?"

"I hope it doesn't have to come to that. Turn around."

He did as he was told and I, in movie style, bashed him with the butt. He was out. I searched and searched finding only ties to use as cuffs and restraints. After he was propped safe in the sofa, I had no fear leaving him alone and went exploring. I passed through each room uninterested. Then there was a study with his collection of books and it was here that I envied his success. Set aside from the rest were his own sitting on a desk juxtaposed to a laptop. Unknowing the password blocked me from getting in but I had a feeling of what was locked away in there.

I picked up one of his books and flipped the leaves of words. Reading few lines here and there I found nothing attractive of his style. Some of it was dry and unmoving. His imagination only created silly stories and nothing left for solid wit and wonder within a pattern. No touch of the soul gripped me while reading. Some points were well written but then left wanting. I tried another book. Then looked at another, finding they were similar with his ridiculous technique.

Dropping the books on the coffee table, the laptop I placed on the chair. He looked like he was still out of it so I didn't bother him. I noticed his fireplace so I decided to light it up. Create a noir atmosphere. I wondered if he knew what noir was. I wondered how the hell he got a deal with such trivial garbage as literature.

For three days neither of us spoke unless it was required or necessary. Being a nice guy I offered him food and drink. He refused but reaching late in the first day asked for a nibble. Seeing as I wouldn't let him loose I had to feed him.

When he first had to use the bathroom he began the dialogue. And I could read his game. I told him I still wasn't untying him. So he had a choice, he could have me help him or piss in his pants. Strange, he chose for the help. He needed to go, I guess. We were very nonchalant about the whole experience. I helped with his pants and he went without complaint. Stared at the floor, the ceiling, his back, his clean bare ass and wondered how it would fly if he had to take a shit. It was crazy to think of such things but here we were. I prayed he didn't have to go number two.

Were there escape attempts? Sure; what victim isn't going to try? Just have to wait for the right opportunities. Once when I went to the bathroom I heard him scuffling around and saw he was hoping to open the door but having a hard time. I began tying his feet after that. There was one where he tried dialing the phone with this his nose and tongue. The line was disconnected after a couple of his efforts amounted to nothing. A sock works well as a muzzle just need something to tie it down with. More ties.

Other than his poor endeavors for freedom and lack of conversation, I filled my time with reading his garbage that he called literature. There was something strange about it; how the language changed at certain moments or even between paragraphs. One moment its good and then nothing. It was driving me nuts. So I decided the only to get rid of this trash was to burn it. Page by page I tore out a leaf and let it fall into the fire watching the words shrink and finally disappearing into ash.

And sleep? I couldn't close my eyes for a minute as I kept guard over this fool. At one point, he pretended to fall asleep in hopes of some telepathic vibe would strike me to follow suit. I yawned but also afraid that if I snoozed he could take advantage of the situation. That couldn't happen, so I kept myself busy by watching television, more reading and shredding, drinking tea, jumping jacks, all trying to keep my body occupied. How long do you have to stay awake for it to be cited as insomnia?

Boredom strikes and your body needs to move. Search and search for things to do that's why I kept myself busy. It's the whole idle hands devil's playthings that I was worried about. And he really had absolutely nothing to do, so I attempted at watching the tube with him. Then he got childish with wanting to switch every channel; couldn't stay on one program. I understood it as trying to rile me up to attempt something stupid. I kept my cool and I left it to where I decided to watch. Though I found things to occupy myself, I could tell he was getting frustrated at not frustrating me.

Holy Thursday—The fourth day wore on like the same nonsense of everyday that had almost became tolerable. I accepted the fact I would never sleep again or leave this house as he recognized me as his captor. So I found a pen, a pad lying around and began writing a little. I worked on some story that hit me about painting a room where the decision for the color was the problem, but the overlapping one. The real issue was underneath between parent and adolescent. I had so much time I figured why not write and I wrote into the night.

"So what's your plan now?" He decided to begin a conversation after dinner. "Is this how we're supposed to live life? I as a captive, you captor. Stuck inside of this house. There'll need to be a point when you need to leave. The food will run out and then what?"

"I don't know. These things, you don't plan out."

"You planned it out pretty well to me."

"I wasn't planning on taking a hostage. Trust me."

He badgered me about making it all the way to him creating this situation. He made it aware that it was me who brought the gun. I tried re-explaining myself but he wouldn't have it. Brushing it aside with his head, he continued with his theories of what he assumed would happen. He stated this era of Beowulf garbage about killing your enemy for self-empowerment. I asked if he believed those things to be true or if anything he read was true. He replied that there was some truth lodged within the pages of fiction.

Then I introduced the truth of our predicament that was lodged in my mind. The word doppelganger sailed through the air into his ear. He laughed. Each breath resonated like the bass pumping in a car bouncing in my chest. His eyes teared up and he wiped his face on the arm of the sofa. My head began its achy-ness again. The fever was still not yet over and the drowse was weighing on me as I tried to steer away from it. Everything seemed to be converging at this one particular moment. My illness, this faker, my loss of dreams, this trip; all of it was coming here.

"So you think I'm the doppelganger. That's perfect considering *I'm* the one being held prisoner."

"Just cause you're the prisoner doesn't mean I'm the evil one. You're the one ruining *my* life." My tone was weak and fearful like a child explaining what's wrong with the adult but getting nowhere. *Tell him.* "You're the opposite of me. You're older and have a home. You're making money and I'm losing mine. You've written books and been successful. I have yet to be published." I knew it was pointless but I had to try. He had to know.

But he continued his laughter. My teeth clenched almost breaking. More pounding within my brain began hitting me in my soul. And I couldn't stand it anymore; I wanted to cry but then he'd know he won. So I left to the bathroom. And there he was staring me down. He was pissed.

"What?" I said to myself. *He's tearing you down you little bitch.* "What would you have me do?" *I told you I was coming out if you wouldn't do what needs to be done.* "And how do you plan on doing that since you're in there?" as I pointed to the mirror.

The wall liquefied as an upright pool. And just as *Stargate*, my other self came right through with ease. He grabbed me and ecstasy began pouring inside. Completeness came over me; this savage taking over of my thoughts, my mannerisms and it seemed my Hyde was coming into play. My mind process changed while it was still me doing everything. I felt power; I felt good. Sinister eyes glared back and a smirk appeared.

Upon reentering I pulled him close giving him two swift slaps and the laughter died out quickly. That fear of his returned and this time I had no gun. It was lying on the chair which he couldn't get to. But that fear returned and I smiled. I thought about slapping him one more time but his only defense was conversation.

"You know anything about xenia?" he shot out.

I shrugged. It didn't matter to me. I was going in one more time but stopped.

"You asked if I believed in anything I read...well...this is something *you* should believe in."

He informed me that it was a Greek custom, ancient, showing hospitality to strangers, travelers, and he was only following that custom. I, like Paris, had broken that relationship and it's a violation to the gods. In doing so, Zeus would punish me. And with that, the room began to heat up as the sweat rolled off his face. It said he was nervous. His voice, on the other hand, resounded in power; the attempt at gaining the upper hand was a quest that would end in failure. I was scared to do anything. Now I was prepared.

"So Polybus," he began. "What do we do now?"

"What'd you call me?"

"Polybus. One of Penelope's suitors, minor character killed by another minor character. Not even worth Odysseus' time."

I laughed and slapped him again. My skin was too bricked for his attempt to get under. The excitement of his cowering filled me with energy to become something, to do something and I knew not what. I restated what I wanted from him. His reply was he had a contract to fulfill. I hit him again. Tears now and not sweat rolled down his face. I had slapped him back to childhood.

"Oh God," he said through his tears. "I was expecting something to happen to me. But not this. This is too much."

"What're you talking about?"

"We are...the cause...of our own demise," he whimpered on.

He was an editor turned writer. He sculpted books that made it to Oprah's Book Club and other best-seller lists. Fame was a desire set aside for too long. Picking out the books he thought best, he would hand over a butchered copy saying it was no good, stealing good points and made up his own novel filling out what he needed. And they sold; the books were picked up. The unfortunates never got deals and tried to sue but some couldn't afford lawyers or knew they couldn't win.

"Look at J. K. Rowling. Someone tried to sue her and didn't get anything. You can't beat someone when they're a blockbuster. So I knew if I hit it big no one would be able to touch me."

"What about the bad copies? That could prove something."

"You can't get sued for stealing an idea that's not patented. If there's no patent its just a scared child waiting for protection and attention."

Ruining the dreams of others to satisfy his own. My blood fumed. He knew karma would find a way to get back to him. When I asked how, his response was lame. Living alone with success, to him, was punishment enough. I walked away knowing different.

Good Friday—The burning flame of the fireplace exemplified the hatred at this point. I continued to toss in papers. The aroma of smoldering pages filled the room as if it were a bouquet lending itself to the décor. Silence, we'd been sitting in it lingering for almost a good few hours. It acted like a blanket of fear for him and for me a pot boiling, simmering, waiting for what may come next. Smells and sound go hand in hand like lovers in heat with candles and music and this is just the foreplay before the act.

The power light of the laptop pulsated with a heartbeat in worry of its own destiny seeing books being torched. The laptop perceived its time drawing to a close. It preferred sleep mode unwanting to experience the eventual fate. So it rested there on the coffee table alone.

"Can I use the bathroom?"

I replied affirmatively and he asked for me to untie his legs so that I wouldn't have to carry him up the stairs. While bending on a knee, I began taking off the ties while he discussed how he hadn't used the toilet for a few days and he felt bloated so he had to go number two. I didn't want to think about wiping his ass so I concentrated on the knots which seemed to have slacked up a bit over time. It must have been the pressure pushing them out, stretching pushing them to loosen.

As I rose to help him up, his hands, that had gotten free, began attacking me. I was caught in a daze by a sudden knock on my chest. The wind left my lungs like a bird firing off in flight. I fell over the coffee table and grabbing the laptop, heaved it at him which missed and smashed against the fireplace. But I used my legs and tripped him up. He fell over and I knew he was reaching for the gun on my chair. I moved to get on top of him and he turned to attack me. Anything he did to hurt me I couldn't feel while I focused on my own assault.

He got up and away and I followed after him. Stumbling through the house trying to find somewhere to go, he didn't think to go outside. Maybe he was trying to defend his home cause he kept throwing whatever he could. But didn't want to leave his house. As he was getting away from me I could see his hands briefly passing over his furniture, pictures, ceramic novelties before tossing them at me. And he ran through the house touching, as you would a lover, all his possessions. Like he was saying farewell. We eventually made it back to the living room and had a bout before I pushed him to the fireplace and grabbed the gun. His back hit the stone and he fell to the floor. When he looked up, he paused.

"Look, hear me out," he whimpered as he stared down the barrel. "I know I was wrong for stealing but killing me is unfair."

"I have nothing to do with you stealing other people's work. You stealing, destroying *my* dreams. If they couldn't get to you, that's their problem."

"I can help you. I've got connections; I know people." He slowly got up. "I can edit your work so that it'll be great."

"Oh yeah," I said sarcastically.

"I can teach you what you need to know about writing. I can be a mentor. My services in exchange for my life?"

In movies, mostly westerns I think, there's always a slight pause where the man with the gun thinks about the proposition. Debating whether it would be a good idea to accept. It rarely happens. The pause is just an effect for the audience. But I live in the real world where no such pause exists. So when he asked, my response was quick.

"As James Joyce told Arnold Bennet, I have nothing to learn from you."

And in movie fashion, I grabbed one of his pillows and slammed it in his face. Pressed the gun up against it and fired off two rounds. A silence fell over the room for a quick second; and in the second life was empty to me. Like there was no soul. Then came a jangled thud and his body lay contorted with no face. Just blood.

Smeared on the stone and on the bullet-holed pillow. Blood. Making a pool around the head and torso. Blood. I felt good.

The corpse held intact for a few seconds before it became a transparent and wispy figment of its former self. It then traveled to the fireplace and danced with ash and cinders that rose. After tenderly kissing the smoke, it flew up and out of the chimney into the early dawn.

The fatigue of restlessness drove me to the couch and pass out. There I was again staring at myself. He who was me smiled with his arms folded. I walked up to him asking what was going on. He replied that there was nothing more for him to do. That it was over. While my body exorcized the fever, he was slowly disappearing himself. He reassured me he'd always be there when I needed him so his disappearance wouldn't matter. This frightened me a little. To know some part of my mind could be so vicious. But I am man and we all have the same tendencies.

When I awoke there was no corpse, no blood, no fever. The house was still in disarray and no reason to clean it up. I made sure the doors and windows were closed and locked. So leaving the week's trouble behind, I exited the tomb of my rival and directed my journey back to the train station. One thing on my mind, home.

Riding the rails, I thought about myself and where my life would head now. In my foolishness, I was still carrying a gun. What's life, I guess, without a little murder? We all think about it from time to time. Same with suicide; it depends if we can justify it. As a human being, I guess what I did could be seen as cruel and wrong. But deep down, as a writer, I had done what was right by our community. There is no more to say on that subject except there is no redemption for myself. This I have accepted. It may take my lifetime to make up for what I've done but there will be no resurrection of me. And so on the ride home, I deduced to drop the gun off in the East River after I've cleaned off prints. Not stupid of course.

I didn't know really what to do. I had no job, little money, no girlfriend, no book deal. In these cases, someone would off himself. I have done that in a way. But I had my health back; my sanity returned to me, even if it is a little distorted now. I felt renewed. A new sense of life entered into my being. What I did know was that I had a chance to start again. There may be no resurrection but the thought of reincarnation of the self illuminated in me. To be different than who I was. But all that comes with experience. Every day we learn something new; we change from the day before so we are reincarnated. And this would be how I restart my life. Press reset and start the game once more. This time I'd know some tricks and codes to get by. I just had to start somewhere. My room. I decided to paint my room white to start fresh, start new. A blank canvas to create a new path. I'd still write of course but with a new sense of conviction. And that made me smile more than any smile I've ever had.

16 June 2009